DICKENS'S CLASS CONSCIOUSNESS:
A MARGINAL VIEW

Dickens's Class Consciousness: A Marginal View

Pam Morris

St. Martin's Press   New York

All rights reserved. For information, write:
Scholarly and Reference Division,
St. Martin's Press, Inc., 175 Fifth Avenue
New York, N. Y. 10010

First published in the United States of America in 1991

Printed in Great Britain

ISBN 0–312–05353–3

Library of Congress Cataloging-in-Publication Data
Morris, Pam 1940–
    Dickens's class consciousness: a marginal view/Pam Morris.
    p. cm.
    Includes bibliographical references (p.) and index.
    ISBN 0–312–05353–3
    1. Dickens, Charles, 1812–1870 — Political and social views.
2. Class consciousness in literature. 3. Social classes in
literature.   I. Title.
PR4592.S58M67   1991
823'. 8–dc20
                                              90–8900
                                                 CIP

To Colin, Vicky, Adam

Contents

Preface and Acknowledgements

In the well-known Preface to the popular edition of *Nicholas Nickleby* (1848), Dickens wrote of himself as a 'not very robust child, sitting in bye-places near Rochester Castle, with a head full of PARTRIDGE, STRAP, TOM PIPES, and SANCHO PANZA'. That insistent picking out of the servants and leaving unmentioned their masters always seems to me significant. Perhaps this is because, when I discovered Dickens for the first time, as an adult, it was his lesser characters rather than his heroes and heroines who obsessed me; figures like Sam Weller, Sairey Gamp, Jenny Wren and even Uriah Heep, filled me with an excitement I found hard to explain. This was not in any sense a response to comic eccentricity; as I examined it, I came to feel that I shared with them a knowledge, a way of seeing the world. There was, within Dickens's texts, a consciousness with which I identified and which I recognized even though I had never fully articulated it. It is a way of seeing which belongs to the experience of marginalization – of both class and sex.

My use of theory has been to provide a conceptual framework as a means of making this personal response rigorous and shareable. Mikhail Bakhtin's analysis of the novel as an inherently dialogic form, always engaged in a polemical relation with dominant voices of its era, offers a means of historicizing texts dynamically, erasing that mechanistic gap between fiction on the one hand and its 'background' on the other. This idea of dialogic interaction also helped me conceptualize my sense of Dickens's novels as dangerous places, inscribed with urgency and passion, his very words saturated with contentiousness. In addition, Bakhtin's argument that novelistic language constructs 'speech images' – linguistic materializations of ideological points of view – coincides with my own sense of the characters mentioned above. Moreover, the concept of 'speech image' allows for formal discussion of character without inference of inner motivation or thought as if they were real individuals. I have centred this study upon a series of characters who, in the phrase Dickens used to describe his younger self, are all represented as 'young Cains'. They are all, to a greater or lesser extent, shaped in early life by city streets.

My aim has been to analyze the relationship of each of these characters to her or his own discourse to discover how far their language offers possibilities and resources for self-making, or to what extent it has become the means of a repressive class interpellation. To explain this constitution of individuals as class subjects I have utilized the work of Lacan and Althusser. However, I have not felt bound by the inherent pessimism of their theories, and throughout my reading of the novels I have attempted to develop a positive as well as a negative hermeneutic. Finally, I should stress that my title is not intended to exclude the *un*conscious, far from it. But neither have I assumed that Dickens carried the knowledge he makes concrete in literary forms wholly locked away from consciousness. We all carry around stores of unarticulated personal experience which we may only recognize as knowledge when we meet it materialized on the page as we read or write.

In this work I have been helped and encouraged by many people. Particular thanks are due to my PhD supervisor at Edinburgh University, Dr Peter Keating; and to Professor K. J. Fielding who has continued to offer most generous support and advice. Like all scholars in Edinburgh I am grateful to the National Library of Scotland which provided such a civilized and efficient place for research. An earlier and lasting debt is to the students and teachers of the Open University; as for so many of its students, it has quite literally changed my life. Throughout the writing of this book my friends and colleagues among Open University tutors, especially Liz Allen, Stewart Hamblyn and Jeremy Tambling, have been an unfailing source of fresh ideas, theoretical expertize, critical rigour, fellowship, and solidarity. To the sisterly support of Jeanette King, also of the Open University, who patiently read and offered helpful and imaginative comments on all my drafts, and to my husband who did likewise, I owe more than I can ever say. Naturally, I am responsible for remaining errors and deficiencies.

P.M.
July 1989

Note on Editions

References to *David Copperfield*, *Dombey and Son*, *Martin Chuzzlewit*, *Oliver Twist* and *Pickwick Papers* are to the Clarendon edition (1966–); all other references to Dickens's works are to the New Oxford Illustrated Dickens (1947–58). Page references are given thus (362). The following editions were used for Dickens's letters, speeches and journalism and are cited subsequently in abbreviated form: *The Letters of Charles Dickens*, ed. by Madeline House, Graham Storey and Kathleen Tillotson, Pilgrim edition (Oxford, 1965–); *The Speeches of Charles Dickens*, ed. by K. J. Fielding (Oxford, 1960); *Uncommercial Traveller and Reprinted Pieces*, New Oxford Illustrated Dickens (1958).

Christian Observer was not published by volume number; monthly editions were bound at the end of each year under the appropriate date and with pages numbered consecutively throughout. References are made therefore by means of the year and page. *Methodist Magazine* has the full title: *The Wesleyan Methodist Magazine* (1828–) being a continuation of the *Arminian* or *Methodist Magazine* first published by John Wesley. Volume numbering is confusing since there are two: one according to the series and one from the beginning of publication. Since page numbering is consecutive yearly from January through to December, I have identified references by year and page only to avoid cluttering the text. *Westminster Review* and *Edinburgh Review* are cited as usual by volume and year.

Introduction: From Margin to Centre

At a banquet honouring 'Literature and Art' given in Birmingham on 2 January 1853, Dickens stood up to express his gratitude for the presentation made to him. It must have been an emotionally charged moment – he was still only forty-one – to have been chosen as the most fitting representative of what was generally regarded as the nation's proudest cultural tradition. What he said on such an occasion would reach into, even if in oblique form, his most deeply-felt aspirations and desires. After speaking for only a few minutes, he referred specifically to those in his audience who were working class, declaring that the honour conferred on him that evening would have given pain instead of pleasure were he not able to assure them 'that what the working people have found me towards them in my books, I am throughout my life . . ., [that] whenever I have tried to hold up to admiration their fortitude, patience, gentleness, the reasonableness of their nature, so accessible to persuasion, and their extraordinary goodness one towards another, I have done so because I have first genuinely felt that admiration myself'.[1]

Such moments are absorbed too easily into a totalizing image of Dickens as great writer and public figure; that constitution of him by countless commentaries tending gradually to glaze over discrepancies, cracks, dangers, discontinuities to achieve a unified, coherent object of our knowledge – 'Dickens' – signifying simultaneously work and man. We need to fragment that unifying image to restore to the moment in Birmingham all its passion and danger as a discursive event; to reactivate the conflicting currents of desire and aggression which moved Dickens, the actual speaking subject, as he gazed narcissistically at the admiring listeners he had singled out. That exchange of gaze, between a man self-made from shameful origins and those he especially addressed, eager for self-improvement, was fraught with risk of recognition and unmasking – the phantasy of a ringing denunciation, 'You're not a *real* gentleman – You're no different from any of us'. Hence the inherent will to control in his discourse with its impulse to subdue and distance through a patronizing interpellation which transforms the working men he speaks to and of into passive objects of his superior knowledge. They are explained and justified to themselves. The need to patronize is stirred also by narcissistic desire, for the power of patronage is a means of measuring the eminence of self from those who are the objects of the beneficient gaze. Greatness can be experienced only in its lived opposition to the humble. But as Dickens's gaze travelled down that distance, it terminated, inevitably, in identification. The admiring faces turned up towards him were like so many reflections of younger or possible self-images, and so his language, patronizing though it is, is charged with a pulse of desire, a felt passion of sympathy.

The texts of his novels need equally to be released from the mystifying totality of a 'corpus' created by the individual 'genius' of their author, Charles Dickens. They need to be repositioned as material, discursive events; as words jostling against other words, responding to some, mimicking others, antagonistic or co-operative, and all saturated with desire, intent, power and danger, in the multi-vocal dialogue, the heteroglossia, of active social intercouse. Instead of author as unified autonomous individual, we need to see a socially constituted subject, the site of conflicting desire, struggling to produce words within the restricted conditions of possibility imposed on his discourse by himself and by the social structures of his time. For a man with a secret past, all words are inherently confessional, and, given the nature of Dickens's secret, no words could have needed more circumspection than those which dealt with class and politics. Hence Dickens's own internalized censorship reinforced the powerful general taboo on these subjects in Victorian England. When he did speak out, always with care and moderation, as at Birmingham, even then his words could be set aside as not belonging to the permitted 'serious' discourses of political economy, religion, or a liberal education which were the only official voices approved for the handling and containment of these threatening topics.

Far from challenging such rules of exclusion, a long tradition of Dickens criticism contributed the sanction of scholarship to the view that his political thought was impressionistic and unrigorous, and, depending on the critic, either benevolent but naive, or naive and reactionary.[2] Moreover, Dickens's lack of formal, academic education was frequently linked, explicitly or implicitly, to what was generally admired as his remarkable insight into extreme states of individual behaviour and passions. The Leavises' influential study, *Dickens the Novelist* (1970), marked the beginning of increased respect for

Dickens's seriousness as a social critic,[3] and subsequent studies established general recognition that his novels, especially from *Dombey and Son* onwards, showed an ever-increasing awareness of the oppressive influence of social structures. However, there was no direct confrontation in these studies of the earlier 'naive' tradition, and as a result unexamined implications of 'sentimentality', 'reaction', even 'naivety' can still haunt accounts of his fiction. Currently, his work is the focus of increasingly sophisticated theoretical approaches, but as yet, none of these have attempted a serious understanding or reassessment of the political conscious or unconscious represented in his novels.[4]

If naivety is involved it seems more appropriately attributed to the view that anyone who moved from the margin of his society to its centre would not be traced upon at every level by the tensions, contradictions, fears and desires produced by that social formation: that their political conscious and unconscious would not necessarily be inscribed with the central conflicts and aspirations of their historical moment. In *The World, the Text, and the Critic*, Edward Said offers a compelling image of the relations of desire and hate between those at the margin and those at the centre, taken from Frantz Fanon's *The Wretched of the Earth*:

> The zone where the natives live is not complementary to the zone inhabited by the settlers ... The settlers' town is a strongly-built town, all made of stone and steel. It is a brightly-lit town; the streets are covered with asphalt, and the garbage-cans swallow all the leavings, unseen, unknown and hardly thought about ... The settlers' town is a well-fed town; its belly is always full of good things. The settlers' town is a town of white people, of foreigners.
>
> The town belonging to the colonized people, or at least the native town, the negro village, the medina, the reservation, is a place of ill-fame, peopled by men of evil repute. They are born there, it matters little where or how. It is a world without spaciousness; men live there on top of each other, and their huts are built on top of the other. The native town is a hungry town, starved of bread, of meat, of shoes, of coal, of light. The native town is a crouching village, a town on its knees, a town wallowing in the mire. It is a town of niggers and dirty arabs. The look that the native turns on the settlers' town is a look of lust, a look of envy; it expresses his dreams of possession — all manner of possession: to sit at the settler's table, to sleep in the settler's bed, with his wife if possible. The colonized man is an envious man.[5]

Said is discussing the will to power in texts so it is somewhat ironic that this extract could stand as a kind of *mise en abyme* for the relations between a 'naive', self-educated reader and that desired world of an enlightened, highly-educated cultural tradition for which Said's own text is a more than adequate symbol. For such a marginalized reader, Said's text becomes an object of desire, of lust; it offers and yet it withholds (except for those who already belong – are already on familiar terms with Auerbach and Arnold, Swift and Vico) the promise of affiliation to the lofty spaciousness of high culture. But for the reader so interpellated, acknowledgement of the desire to belong to that world, immediately invokes the admission of lack, of an absence in the self of the object of desire. This brings a sense of inadequacy but also a sense of alienation and even hostility. Such a reader wants both to live in the palace of wisdom and to raze it. Fanon's colonized/colonizer relations typify the relations of all forms of marginalization to the centre: a fusion of desire with hostility, of identification with alienation.

II

The work of Louis Althusser and Jacques Lacan provides a useful theoretical framework to explain the constitution and the functioning of this relation.[6] According to Lacan, at the mirror-phase of the infant's development, it achieves a joyful perception of itself as a unified being, physically separate and independent from its surrounding world – an image of itself such as it might indeed see in a mirror. This recognition of a specular image offers a wholly desirable self in contrast to the infant's actual state of total dependence, unco-ordinated motor skills, and boundary uncertainty between itself and the world. It is, however, misrecognition, since self can never be identical to image. Thus the narcissistic desire for a unified self initiated in the mirror stage and pursued throughout life is always for a phantasy, for the imaginary ego-ideal. This first splitting of the subject into a perceiving self and a self as imaged is repeated in the next phase of development – entry into the Symbolic Order. A sense of individual subjectivity is constituted with the acquisition of the first person pronoun singular, but as with the specular image there exists an unclosable gap between the 'I' who speaks and the 'I' which is the subject of that discourse. These two phases of development, the mirror stage and entry into language, constitute the subject's sense of self as an autonomous individual, but, since this image is an imaginary ideal, the subject is decentred and driven always by narcissistic desire after a unified ego-ideal it can never attain.

It is this ceaseless pursuit of a desired self-image that facilitates the social constitution of the subject. Once within the Symbolic Order, a perception of self is mediated by language and the ego-ideal is sought in those social models approved by society. These socially-valorized ideals function rather like magic mirrors, promising to reflect back on those subjects who conform (of their own free will) a sense of unified identity and value. In other words, they function as an Ideal Subject, or as Althusser says, an 'Absolute Subject [who] occupies the unique place of the centre, and interpellates around it the infinity of individuals into subjects in a double mirror-connexion such that it *subjects* the subjects to the Subject'.[7] By offering an ideal image in which to find and contemplate themselves, the Absolute Subject becomes the desired object of subjects who therefore 'willingly' subject themselves to its conformity. However, the desire the Absolute Subject invokes, meets, but fails to satisfy, necessarily implies a lack, and this gap in the mechanism which constitutes subjects provides a point of fracture within the total determinism Althusser seems at times to imply. The interpellation of subjects by Absolute Subject has always a necessary double nature: there is identification with the desired image, but simultaneously alienation from it since what is desired must be lacked. At its extreme, individual subjects recognize themselves in God's image, but that identification involves at the same time a humiliating sense of difference and separation.

III

This model of identification with alienation offers a means of understanding the nature and mechanisms of class marginalization, the patterns of which, psychological and social, inscribe themselves upon Dickens's texts. In the early decades of the nineteenth century, marginalization by class was still a new and harsh experience; it only became the dominant form of social relation with the seizure and consolidation of hegemonic power by the middle class which brought into being the Victorian social formation. At the material base, there was, during the last decades of the eighteenth century and the first decades of the nineteenth century, an accelerating shift of economic power from land to the capitalist class. At the hegemonic level this necessitated a remaking of the imaginary relations of individuals to the real relations in which they lived. From perceiving themselves as positioned, according to family and rank, within a harmonious, well-ordered scheme of being, divinely appointed and unchangingly maintained, subjects came to feel themselves free individuals, at liberty to make their own place and fortune in the world through adherence to the moral virtues of industry, enterprise, and prudent accumulation. From the elitism of birth the notion changed to that of an elitism of individual worth: God would reward the deserving, not the well-born. Thus the change in the imaginary relations of individuals to their world involved a movement away from filiation or family as a source of self-identity to that of affiliation of merit. However, unlike self-evident ties of blood, ties of affiliation need to be defined in opposition to what they are not; an affiliated group can experience its identity only by reference to those who are different and are not of the group. Class affiliation, therefore, depends upon the power to exclude and marginalize, as well as to interpellate.

In the first stages of its struggle for hegemonic ascendancy, the middle class gained a sense of solidarity and identity by defining itself against the aristocracy. In opposition to aristocratic 'vices' of paternalism, parasitism, indolence, and dissolute extravagance, the bourgeoisie asserted the moral virtues of enterprise, diligence, and thrifty sobriety. From the outset, these ideological claims were taken up and validated by two powerful discourses of 'truth': the traditional 'true' discourse of religion, expressed by the rising force of evangelicalism, and the potent new 'true' discourse of empirical science, expressed by the Utilitarians. Thus reason and religion joined forces to insist on the divine and natural superiority of the middle class whose enterprise, energy, and industry had enriched the whole nation.

'It is especially among those very classes, that is, the middle ranks of society, neither the highest or the lowest, that God has been preparing a people to serve him. The middle classes are perhaps, more than any other, within reach of both reason and of scriptural influence' claimed the *Christian Observer*, the main journal of the Established Evangelicals.[8] The *Westminster Review*, the official organ of the Utilitarians, stated a similar view in its very first number: 'Of the political and moral importance of this class, there can be but one opinion. It is the strength of the community. It contains beyond all comparison the greatest proportion of the intelligence, industry and wealth of the nation.'[9] Together, these two discourses of religion and reason constructed a new hegemonic myth of human existence characterized by a strongly causal plot structure. Individual lives were seen as shaped by the inevitable working of divine and economic 'laws' determining the consequence of every action and choice made. 'It has pleased God,' explained the *Christian Observer*, 'to connect cause with effect: we may dislike what we are compelled to see, we may strive to disprove it, but we cannot set it aside: there it is in all its obviousness, and our only course, as Christians and political economists, is to shape our conduct accordingly' (1832, p. 580).

This causal plot of human life presupposes and reinforces the myth of unified individuality; there has to be some essential core of identity to be wrought upon by the causal process. It also reinforces the myth of autonomy since the individual *freely* chooses at each moment in life, even though subjected to the irrevocable consequences of those choices. Even the evangelical belief in election did not weaken the sense of causality. It merely gave it a retrospective sanction, since those whom God had chosen as his elect could be expected to show outward signs of grace in the manner of their living. In Fielding's *Tom Jones*, the plot is structured by contingency; what happens to Tom, whom he meets, and what he does have little bearing upon his final restoration to the place belonging to him by right of birth. In contrast, Lydgate's fate in *Middlemarch*, despite his genteel connections, is rigidly determined at every point by the conjunction of his moral decisions with economic and social 'laws'. In these two paradigmatic plot structures we see the changed imaginary relations of individuals to the real relations in which they lived. Inevitably, these changed imaginary relations brought into being a new Absolute Subject: the idealized image of a free, striving individual, whose high moral worth inevitably resulted in and was reflected by worldly success and social distinction.

The capitulation of birth to the ideological claims of individual worth was hastened by the events of the French Revolution. The aristocracy felt the prudence of identifying its interests with those of the rising capitalist class against the greater danger from below. As Lady Shelley wrote in her diary, 'The awakening of the labouring classes, after the first shocks of the French Revolution, made the upper classes tremble. Every man felt the necessity of putting his house in order'.[10] Despite utilization of apparently democratic interpellations, claiming the rights of the 'people' against the privileges of the aristocratic few, the middle class had no intention of extending the freedom and power it sought any further downwards to the working class it employed. It was imperative, therefore, to find a means of inhibiting any demands for an even greater extension of social and political equality. For this purpose, the myth of divine and economic causation in human life proved to be even more efficacious than in challenging the noble prerogatives of status according to birth. If prosperity and respectability were held to be the inevitable outward signs and consequences of inner moral worth, then it followed that those who failed in the competitive struggle to make a living and succeed were morally unfit. Belief in Samuel Smiles' assertion in *Self-Help*, 'What some men are, all without difficulty might be. Employ the same means, and the same result will follow',[11] provided a comforting glow of self-approbation for the well-to-do, but was a bleak judgement of personal inadequacy on those already suffering the physical hardships of poverty. Increasingly, after the French Revolution, the middle class defined its identity, not in opposition to the aristocracy, but in marginalization of the working class. Growing wealth, increasing employment of servants, extended education, all helped sharpen the sense of difference. Despite public approval for the 'respectable poor', it was in fact upon vociferous reiterations of the uncouth behaviour and moral degeneracy of the 'vulgar poor' that the middle class depended to construct their sense of class identity and worth. Rough hands, uneducated speech, unpolished manners became reliable signifiers of inner spiritual coarseness, and absolutely necessary as such to define and justify bourgeois hegemony.

The discourses of religion and reason were as assiduous in constituting and maintaining the myth of the inevitable causation of poverty in moral laxity as they had been in constructing the plot of worldly success as a consequence of individual moral virtue. From its very first number in 1824, the *Westminster Review*, in recurrent articles on the poor laws, on emigration, on charity, on factory legislation, asserted that working-class people were essentially immoral, improvident, and lazy. A review in January 1837 clearly sums up this myth of the guilty poor: 'Nor are the industrious ... often found among the destitute even in old age. The poorest of the poor (speaking of the mass) are necessarily either the most ignorant, or the most improvident, or the most intemperate, or the class of criminals' (4 (1836–7), p. 370). To this reasoning the evangelicals added a pervasive sense of sin. The doctrine of the total depravity of human nature fitted snugly with the 'laws' of political economy and surplus population. It was but a short step from there to the view that poverty was ordained by God as punishment for moral degeneracy – the earthly badge of shame and suffering to mark his displeasure and to bring the recipient of divine wrath, through this harsh discipline, to penitence and a new life. To disrupt this causal plot structuring human life by relieving poverty was thus to obstruct the will of Providence: 'The natural and divinely ordained punishment for indolence or improvidence is want; if they will not work, neither shall they eat; and no stronger stimulus to industry is requisite, unless meddling legislation has deranged what God ordained' (*Christian Observer*, 1832, p. 850). It is essential always to bear in mind that for the whole of the nineteenth century, due to the precarious conditions of working-class life, the terms 'poor' and 'working class' are interchangeable. Any misfortune – illness, trade depressions, market fluctuations – would plunge even the most respectable working-class families into extreme poverty, and all faced destitution in old age.

Most obviously these causal arguments consolidated the confidence of the middle class in its own divine and natural right to affluence and power. However, despite this, the imaginary Absolute Subject constituted by the myth of individual worth exercised a seductively open and classless interpellation. By this means it was able to maintain a powerful influence for social control over those it actually marginalized and excluded. The ideal image of material success and respectability as the reflection and reward of inner worth is never logically closed off to desire even for the poor. Underpinned by the paradigmatic plot of individual freedom working in conjunction with the causal necessity of divine and natural laws, the Absolute Subject holds out a perpetual promise of ultimate identification: behave like this, conform to this image, and affiliation to respectability must follow – eventually! However, as in all relations of margin to the centre, this interpellation has a double nature. Desire to identify with the Absolute Subject subjects the will to social conformity, but this is buttressed by the Subject's power of intimidation. The greater the distance of margin to centre, of self from ego-ideal, the greater the force of desire, but the greater the desire, the greater must be the subject's lack. For the mass of the working class, for the social failures and misfits of Victorian England, the distance of themselves from their desired image was a measure of their own inferiority and unworth. Hence a demoralizing sense of their own unfitness imposed a powerful inhibition upon the claims of the marginalized for greater social justice, and helped mask that dangerous split between desire and alienation inherent in interpellation of periphery to centre.

IV

Dickens, of course, was in no sense working-class, but his early and most deeply-felt experience in life was of the marginalization of social failure, the shame of poverty, and the stigma of unskilled labour. During that early time, he lived close to the working-class culture of city streets, whose influence he claimed had shaped his imagination; an assertion he reiterated throughout his life.[12] In moving so rapidly from that marginalization to a position of esteem at the centre, Dickens experienced the contradictions inherent in interpellation of margin to centre in extreme form: intense desire for narcissistic identification with social images of success and respectability, fused with a deep fear of personal lack, in turn stimulating an alienated, hostile perspective on the object of desire.

This fusion of desire with hate, identification with alienation, invests every aspect of Dickens's texts with a dialogic tension. In his fiction, the various character discourses construct what Bakhtin calls 'speech images': materializations of ideological points of view or ways of seeing the world.[13] Frequently, these voices or 'speech images' articulate class perspectives, as Dickens himself acknowledged when he suggested readers should substitute classes for his individual fictitious characters.[14] These contending voices, materializing hegemonic and non-hegemonic marginalized viewpoints, are brought into a dialogic relation in Dickens's texts, and thus articulate those oppositional voices and ideological antagonisms of the era, silenced within dominant discourse. This internal polemical dialogism extends, also, into the imaginary 'solutions' the narratives construct for the social problems inscribed within them, so that the resolution of the main story is often implicitly challenged by values asserted in the subtext. This intrinsic dialogism is most clearly demonstrated at the level of plot structure. From *Martin Chuzzlewit* onwards all the novels conform, to a greater of lesser extent, to the hegemonic plot of moral causality. In each text one or more of the major characters traces a course of individual moral progress, frequently paralleled by a progress towards financial security and respectability as well. *David Copperfield* and *Great Expectations* show this causal plot structure most starkly, but Mr Dombey's life is also shaped by a moral pattern of cause and effect, as is Mr Gradgrind's, Sidney Carton's, and Bella Wilfer's. These moral plots express a desire to identify with the ideal of moral respectability.

However, at a deeper level the novels are structured by older plot patterns which implicitly challenge the hegemonic claims of the moral plot. At the centre of each story, from *Oliver Twist* onwards, is a tangle of illegitimacy or illicit love, often both, which acts as a catalyst bringing together characters from all social levels, and eventually revealing the hidden bonds of their shared humanity. This underlying structure of what could be called a social sub-plot involves minor characters as much as major ones, and may even shift the focus of the novel centrifugally away from the centre towards the margin. Oliver Twist is the child of seduction and illicit love and as a result of this origin in shame, he becomes involved in misadventures which bring such securely respectable members of society as Mr Brownlow and Rose Maylie into personal contact with the subterranean world of thieves, murderers and prostitutes. In *Nicholas Nickleby*, the outcast Smike turns out to be the son of a secret marriage contracted by wealthy Ralph Nickleby. Another social outcast, Hugh, in *Barnaby Rudge*, leader of the mob which attacks the homes of the wealthy, is revealed to be the illegitimate son of Sir John Chester and a gypsy woman hanged at Tyburn. In *Dombey and Son*, Alice Marwood's desire for revenge on Carker who exploited her poverty to seduce and ruin her, forces Mr Dombey into terms of familiarity with the degraded figure of Good Mrs Brown. In *David Copperfield*, the different classes are linked again by the exploitative passion of Steerforth for Em'ly, and this explicit treatment is returned to in *Our Mutual Friend*. Meanwhile, in *Little Dorrit*, the guilty family secret which involves Clennan with the world of the Marshalsea turns out to be illicit love and illegitimacy.

Whereas in eighteenth-century novels illegitimacy frequently functions within the narrative pattern to reassert an underlying orderliness in the social and natural universes, in Dickens's texts it serves the opposite purpose, rupturing a falsely imposed order to reveal underlying areas of guilt and shame. The Victorian middle class constructed its identity upon an absolute opposition between its respectability and the moral unfitness of the working class. Despite this, it was hidden, unstated, but generally known that the most common and certainly the most intimate contact between the classes was through prostitution and seduction. This vast, unspoken sexual exploitation of the labouring poor was related causally to the frigid code of respectability and to the insistence that marriage be delayed until prosperity was assured. These, however, were causal truths ruthlessly excluded from the hegemonic myth of individual moral and economic progress. There was a similar causal link between the plentiful supply of poor women to meet the sexual needs of their social superiors and the abject poverty of the working class, and especially of working women, many of whom, like milliners and lace-makers, could only avoid actual starvation by supplementing their wages through prostitution.[15] Economic facts like this were well-known and constantly threatened to erode that boundary of difference between the classes so necessary to the middle-class sense of separate identity and righteous justification. Thus the structuring motifs of illegitimacy and illicit love in Dickens's texts provide a powerfully emotive image by which to express the fundamentally exploitative nature of class relations and of the intimacy of their contact – truths which the middle class, like Podsnap in *Our Mutual Friend*, sought to sweep from the face of the earth. However, the very secrecy of the relationship gave the image its generalized effect; the most proper families could feel vulnerable to the threat of a sudden revelation which might link them by blood with those they affected to despise as morally degenerate. 'Bone of his bone, flesh of his flesh, shadow of his shadow' – thus Mrs Snagsby in her relation with Mr Snagsby, but flesh is not kept inviolable by a marriage ceremony leading only to the frigid respectability of her bed. The shadow which haunts her life, as she haunts her husband's, is the spectre of disgrace in the form of Jo, wretched outcast of society – but somebody's child. As Alice Marwood's mother insists, 'There's relationships without your clergy and your wedding rings – they may make it, but they can't break it' (784).

The Victorian working class called themselves the 'bastards' of society and their position was similar to that of Oliver Twist, labelled by his shameful birth 'the humble, half-starved drudge – to be cuffed and buffeted through the world – despised by all and pitied by none' (3). Illegitimacy, therefore, fuses together in one image the two areas of bourgeois guilt: the brutal exploitative relations of labour and of sex imposed on the poor. The terror, guilt, and remorse which overwhelm Ralph Nickleby when he discovers that the wretched outcast Smike, harried to death by poverty and ill-treatment, is his own son, gives expressive form to the uneasy conscience hidden beneath the apparent security of the Victorian class structure. Dick Swiveller, in *The Old Curiosity Shop*, creeping down the back stairs, finds what was literally the skeleton in the middle-class cupboard – a starved and beaten little servant who is also the illegitimate daughter of Sally Brass and Quilp. It is a perfect piece of symbolism, exposing the truth 'below stairs' of Victorian society.

Thus, an older structural form of mysterious birth, common to fairy and folk tale, articulates the latent hostility of a marginalized view; that impulse to unmask, even violate, the object of desire – genteel respectability. In the later novels this structural motif becomes more complex still, through interrelation with a second subversive underlying narrative element. This involves a pattern of doomed circular flight, in which illicit love and illegitimacy centre increasingly upon the impossibility of escape from one's past, from shame, guilt, and the physical force of sexual desire. Again and again in these novels the hegemonic myth of causal progress is challenged, as origins assert their physical claims, and men and women are forced to recognize the impossibility of flight from the bondage of their own flesh into the frozen safety of genteel posturing. William Dorrit's journey from the shame of the Marshalsea to the imprisoning sterility of the Alps, with its museum of frozen corpses, and then downwards towards his ultimate social humiliation provides a symbolic paradigm of the doomed flight structure. Lady Dedlock traces a similar path from her posture of icy hauture to her identification in death with the poor beaten wife of the brickmaker. She dies at the entrance of the paupers' graveyard where Nemo, the father of her child, is buried, his name denoting a similar loss of social identity. As the narrator insists in *Dombey and Son*, 'In this round world of many circles within circles, do we make a weary journey from the high grade to the low, to find at last that they lie close together, that the two extremes touch, and that our journey's end is but our starting place' (477). This too is the structural form of *Great Expectations*, in which Pip's aspirations are brought back to earth by the materialization of his past and his shame in the repulsive figure of a returned convict. Estella, in whose proud cold beauty Pip found the mirroring realization of his desire for gentility, is revealed, through an inverse parody of fairy-tale transformation, as the daughter of Magwitch and a murderess.

Clearly, as well as expressing that urge to unmask respectability, this obsessive pattern articulates the return of Dickens's fear of unmasking; his unappeasable anxiety that his own lack would be recognized and marked with public scorn, just as Merdle in *Little Dorrit* is recognized and stigmatized by his butler. However, the circular flight structure is more polysemic than this. In the oldest forms of cyclical narrative, the return to origins is always regenerative, moving through death into a renewal of life. In Dickens's later fiction the notion of resurrection is treated most explicitly in *A Tale of Two Cities*, but in all the late novels the circular flight structure is linked to a search for regeneration in origins. The precise extent to which this intrinsic and often subversive dialogism of Dickens's texts is expressing a political conscious or unconscious is probably unresolvable and not important; the separation of conscious from unconscious is without sharp boundary and in any case always on the move.

V

A dialogic reading practice is essential for the accentuation of these complex internal polemics. A dialogic approach also allows for some redistribution of critical focus from the central characters, at times the least imaginatively compelling, towards those at the margin of the text. Often these are represented as at the social margin too, and while their depiction, as we shall see, is deeply-rooted in the actual culture of city streets, they owe least to realist forms of art. The representation of these characters draws freely upon traditional elements in folk and popular art: parody, grotesquerie, visual and verbal comedy, and theatricality. In this, they contrast with the main characters whose presentation usually conforms to realist conventions, in keeping with their function within the ideological 'solutions' put forward by the causal moral plot.

The texts also need to be read in terms of an external dialogism to restore to them their unsettling, unfinished quality as discursive events. Only by reinserting them in the dialogues in which they engage is it possible to re-energize their challenge, their passion, and their signifying silences — just as we need to re-articulate the illegitimacy motif within the lived conditions and fears of Victorian class and sexual relations. Ideally one should re-accentuate every voice raised during the production of a text; obviously an impossible task. The main focus of this study is the way Dickens's texts express, explore, and challenge the social and psychological effects of interpellation of margin to centre in a class formation with the resulting constitution of individuals as class subjects. Since the most powerful and authoritative voices involved in this hegemonic activity were the 'true' discourses of religion and reason as expressed by the evangelical and Utilitarian movements, Dickens's texts are read largely, but not exclusively, in dialogic relation to these voices. This is not intended as a study of Dickens's views on evangelicalism and Utilitarianism, but of the interaction of the novels with hegemonic discourse. Neither is it implied that Dickens necessarily read the journals referred to and literally replied to them. The most widely-read and influential publications of these two movements are used because they provide the nearest we can get now to the actual generalized public discourses they generated, and to the changing inflection of these dominant voices over time and in response to material events. Hegemonic power is not a monolithic static system of domination, but a continuous process of shifting emphasis, accommodation, struggle, and appropriation among the various class sections of any social formation. It is with the dominant hegemonic voices within this interactive heteroglossia that Dickens's novels engage politically, not with the underlying beliefs and philosophy of evangelicalism and Utilitarianism.[16]

This engagement is not expressed solely as a negative reaction. To read Dickens's texts is always to recognize that they are inscribed with passionate currents of desire. Hence alienation from the valorized ideal of individual progress does not lead only to the urge to unmask and violate. There is also a displacement of desire towards another ideal image offering unity and plenitude to the self. Dickens's texts articulate an alternative utopian impulse. They construct an affirmative vision of human life in terms of community, in which constitution of subjects is shown as co-operative process rather than the closure of individualism. This opposing ideal to the hegemonic Absolute Subject springs from the material conditions of lived experience in the city streets and imprints itself most firmly upon the early novels.

Notes

1. *Speeches*, p. 155.
2. The 'benevolent but naive' tradition begins as early as 1904 in Louis Cazamian's *The Social Novel in England 1830–1850* (1973), where Dickens's political thought is described as a 'vague and sentimental form of Christian socialism' (p. 243). Edmund Wilson's otherwise seminal essay, 'Dickens: The Two Scrooges' (1941) reproduces this critical blind spot, declaring that 'fundamentally [Dickens] was not interested in politics' (rpt. in *The Wound and the Bow*, 1961, p. 25), and this judgement remains implicit in Barbara Hardy, *The Moral Art of Dickens* (1970). Humphrey House, in *The Dickens World* (1941), sought to adjust the 'benevolent' view of Dickens with an emphasis on the strictly bourgeois values the novels assert, a tradition continued by Philip Collins in his influential *Dickens and Crime* (1962) and *Dickens and Education* (1963). This 'reactionary and naive' Dickens is constituted most fully in John Carey, *The Violent Effigy* (1973).
3. F. R. and Q. D. Leavis, *Dickens the Novelist* (1970). Also influential in insisting upon Dickens's seriousness as a social critic was John Lucas, *The*

Melancholy Man: A Study of Dickens's Novels (1970).

4. The nearest approach to this is Michael Hollington, *Dickens and the Grotesque* (1984), which argues convincingly that Dickens uses the grotesque to construct a satiric critique of his society. However, Hollington's focus is necessarily upon the rhetoric of the grotesque in the fictions rather than their political acumen. Myron Magnet, *Dickens and Social Order* (1985), claims to re-present the 'reactionary' argument for a 'thinking' conservative 'Hobbesian' Dickens, but his textual evidence for this is strangely selective. Meanwhile, Alexander Welsh, *From Copyright to Copperfield* (1987) has tilted interest away from political readings altogether, mounting a persuasive argument that Dickens's early experience of social shame in the blacking warehouse has been over-emphasized by his critics.

5. Quoted in Said (1984), p. 49. This quotation from *The Wretched of the Earth* by Frantz Fanon is reprinted by kind permission of Grafton Books.

6. In what follows I draw largely upon the ideas contained in Jacques Lacan, *Ecrits: A Selection*, translated by Alan Sheridan (1980), and Althusser's essay 'Ideology and Ideological State Apparatuses' in Louis Althusser, *Essays in Ideology* (1984), pp. 1–60.

7. Althusser, p. 54.

8. *Christian Observer*, 1833, p. 21. Subsequent references to this journal will be indicated in the text. Throughout, the usual practice is adopted of indicating Evangelicals within the established church by use of a capital E, whilst the much larger body of those who subscribed generally to evangelical beliefs is referred to without a capital letter.

9. *Westminster Review*, 1 (1824), p. 68. Subsequent references will be indicated in the text. Throughout, I use a capital U to refer to any individual or group subscribing to Utilitarian views, as well as to those closely identified with Bentham's circle, in order to distinguish between this specialized use of the word to indicate a way of thinking and its general usage in the language.

10. Quoted in E. P. Thompson, *The Making of the English Working Class* (Harmondsworth, Middlesex, 1968), p. 60.

11. *Self-Help*, (1958 edition), p. 284.

12. For example, struggling with *Dombey and Son* while in Switzerland, he felt his problems in writing arose from 'the absence of streets and numbers of figures. I can't express how much I want these. It seems as if they supplied something to my brain, which it cannot bear, when busy, to lose' (*Letters*, IV, 612–13).

13. Mikhail Bakhtin, *The Dialogic Imagination*, edited by Michael Holquist, translated by Carol Emerson and Michael Holquist (University of Texas Press, 1981), pp. 259–422, but see especially pp. 333, 362–5, and Glossary, p. 429.

14. During his trip to America he told an audience, 'I feel as though we are agreeing – as indeed we are, if we substitute for fictitious characters the

classes from which they are drawn' (*Speeches*, p. 21).

15. For a full discussion of the sexual relations between classes see Steven Marcus, *The Other Victorians: A Study of Sexuality and Pornography in Mid-Nineteenth Century England* (1967). See also Frederick Engels, *The Condition of the Working Class in England* (Frogmore, St Albans, Herts., 1969 edition), p. 221.

16. For evangelicalism see Dennis Walder, *Dickens and Religion* (1981). Humphrey House, *The Dickens World* (1942), discusses Dickens and Utilitarianism. See also F. R. & Q. D. Leavis, *Dickens the Novelist* (1970), pp. 187–212.

Part I:
Strategies of Survival

1

The Early Novels: Laughter

It needs a conscious act of historical imagination to read Dickens's early texts now with a fresh perception of the political noise and passions characterizing that decade of the 1830s which produced them. It is too easy to embalm them in a timeless silence. Yet from 1829 to 1832 a severe trade depression and series of bad harvests led to continual outbreaks of violent industrial unrest in the north of England and to revolt all over the agricultural south. In 1830, there were strikes by spinners in Yorkshire and the Midlands, and by miners in Wales, Lancashire, and Yorkshire. From Kent to Dorset a spate or rick-burning and machine-breaking culminated in the hanging of nine agricultural workers and the transportation of 457 others. In 1834, the Tolpuddle Martyrs were sentenced and transported. The passing of the Reform Bill in 1832 and the New Poor Laws in 1834, twin symbols of the hegemonic ascendancy of middle-class individualism, were preceded and accompanied by continuous popular disturbances and violent agitations.

This prolonged atmosphere of simmering unrest in all parts of the country reawakened the spectre of social revolution which haunted the imaginations of the authorities and the well-to-do throughout most of the century following the French Revolution. Doubtless, it was this pressing fear which gave such unity of tone to dominant discourse of the time. 'It is impossible to turn to our manufacturing districts, and survey the vast and dense masses of population which they now contain, without a feeling bordering on alarm,' wrote the *Methodist Magazine* in 1831. It continued, 'Where such immense multitudes of the lower classes are brought into such close contact with each other, and such opportunities are afforded them for the communication of sentiment, and the combination of influence, what could resist them were they to take a wrong direction?'[1] To prevent any such wrong turning the evangelicals and Utilitarians ignored fundamental antagonisms in their philosophies to insist that irrevocable 'laws' of science and religion demonstrated a necessary causal connection between wealth and inner worth, poverty and moral degeneracy. The poor were poor, not because of social injustice, but because of their own sins of profligacy, recklessness, and immorality. To improve their lives, it was not greater political justice they needed, but greater self-restraint.

In 1831, the *Westminster Review* rebuked the Society for the Diffusion of General Knowledge for not producing, as a priority, a pamphlet on the science of political economy for the working class: 'When by this means [political economy] they are made to see the necessity of a strict adherence to morality and law, and are consequently made moral and obedient, and easy in their condition then is the time...to succeed in conveying a knowledge of... physical sciences' (14 (1831), p. 369). In the same year the *Christian Observer* wrote of the desirability of teaching every national school child 'what we may call, the poor man's political economy – his real, not Utopian rights' (1831, p. 240). This sentiment was quickly echoed in the *Methodist Magazine*: 'To complete the system of national education, there should be added instruction on those other subjects which...the "Christian Observer" has well designated "the poor man's political economy"...[with] instruction of this kind...the lower ranks...will be less likely to view the rich and great as oppressors who have unsurped their just rights' (1831, p. 476). From every direction these hegemonic discourses of 'truth' and 'reason' asserted the irrevocable causal plot governing human existence as self-evident fact. Against such divine and natural necessity there could be no appeal, and there was no alternative. By the end of the decade even Carlyle, implacable in his dislike of the 'dismal' sciences, was writing that the old poor laws had provided a 'bounty on unthrift, idleness, bastardy and beer-drinking' and declaring of anyone who would not work, 'let him perish according to his necessity: there is no law juster than that'.[2] And this at a time when Henry Mayhew estimated that three wet days could bring 30,000 people in London alone to the brink of starvation.[3]

If repetition impresses a sense of necessity, then the evangelical magazines must take full credit. A major feature of every issue were biographies of pious and respectable lives, invariably exhibiting a marked causal structure; most frequently of youthful misdemeanour leading to sudden repentance and conversion, followed by a life of diligent endeavour, duty, and watchfulness, usually accompanied by the 'reward' of worldly prosperity as well. Every monthly issue of the

Methodist Magazine contained as many as thirty such biographies, ranging in length from short obituary paragraphs to several detailed pages. Invariably, any accounts illustrating a reverse causal pattern – wilful misbehaviour leading to personal disaster, penury, and deathbed terror – were taken from working-class life. In the cholera epidemic of 1832, the *Methodist Magazine* reprinted lurid descriptions of the deaths of the dissolute, all of whom were of the labouring poor. 'O how this sweeping scourge has cut down the ungodly', it proclaimed (1832, p. 205).

However, as a means of social control, of preventing the working class taking that 'wrong direction', the threat of divine retribution after the act was as nothing compared to the divine ability to penetrate to the deepest core of being of each subject. 'Consider that He knoweth whereof you are made, that He possesses free access to, and irresistible power over, every nerve and fibre of your body', wrote the *Christian Observer* (1841, p. 454). This terrorizing conception of God, constantly reiterated, constructed a 'panoptican' subjectivity inside the individual subject, an internalized process of scrutinizing, monitoring, and judging the most trivial and fleeting thoughts and deeds. 'Let your confessions of sin be full, pointed and personal; attempt no conceal-ment; nothing can be hidden from God', warned the *Methodist Magazine*. It continued:

> [The] awful truth [that] we are continually under the inspection of God ... should rouse our energies, kindle our zeal and excite us to the utmost diligence and care in whatever duty we may be called to engage ... My careless hand may occasionally hang down unperceived by others ... But it is not so with regard to the omniscient God. He knows perfectly well what I can do, and what I ought to do, as well as what I actually do. He detects the smallest failure, and the least omission, and marks it with his disapprobation. 'Thou God seest me' (1841, p. 107).

This internalized, personalized watchfulness was kept constantly on edge by insistence on the 'wholesome doctrine ... of man's total depravity', 'a deep and abiding conviction of our own guilty and lost estate' (*Christian Observer*, 1841, p. 455). What this discourse led to was the creation of a culture of guilt, anxiety, and repressive seriousness, in which subjects were interpellated wholly in terms of work, duty, and self-distrust. Any relaxation, any activity almost, apart from work and submissive prayer, was seen as a revealing indication of moral laxity. In the pages of the evangelical journals, even the simplest pleasure became 'another step downwards in that precipitous and slippery path which conducts to the blackness of darkness for ever' (*Christian Observer*, 1836, p. 389). Solemn warnings were issued against frivolity in dress, conversation, or manner, against wandering thoughts, undue familiarity with friends or family, intemperance, idle moments, and every and any 'gratification of the flesh'. 'While genuine religion . . . promotes our happiness . . . there is much in it tending to produce a deep seriousness of spirit, and an ungloomy but real solemnity of manner. The Christian sees the real character of life. It is a warfare and a pilgrimage', wrote the *Methodist Magazine* (1831, p. 552).

Any outlet for the imagination was regarded with the gravest suspicion as affording a potential means of escape from this constant repressive self-regimentation. Theatres and novels, especially in their effect upon the young, were regarded as unmitigated evil, leaving their victims 'weakened – wearied – unfitted for ordinary employments, and sick of sober realities' (*Christian Observer*, 1831, p. 424). One correspondent to the *Christian Observer* felt that especially in books intended for the lower classes, there should be 'a total abstinence from tales of mysterious wonder' so that such readers would be taught to 'reason and reflect instead of cherishing vague wonder' (1833, p. 654). 'Truth and truth alone', wrote another Gradgrind evangelical, 'is the wholesome food'. By contrast, imagination is 'corrupt in its root' and 'pernicious in its operation', leading the mind away from the moral lessons of the 'true and often heart-withering realities of life' (*Christian Observer*, 1836, p. 455). The young were the especial focus of such doctrines. Evangelical insistence that children were born into sin was only statement of ideological fact. They acquired their sense of guilt with their name and their language. Indeed, the process of self-repression could begin even before full entry into the Symbolic Order:

As a commencement of my plan, I deemed it necessary to ascertain the earliest moment at which the infant was capable of understanding my frown . . . The advantages resulting were that unnecessary crying was prevented, and a habit of submission formed . . . Hence it will be seen that the twig was bent in its earliest growth; and the blessing of the Lord could not be withheld, where prayer was so accompanied by unceasing watchfulness (*Methodist Magazine*, 1836, p. 752).

For sin, Utilitarians substituted the vigilance of competition. Life was to be seen as a struggle for individual success, each against each, spurred on by fear of failure. The praise for the Lancastrian system of education in the first issue of the *Westminster Review* gives clear expression to the Utilitarian vision of a docile, productive population with each subject individualized but isolated in a competitive watchfulness of all other:

> The grand moral advantage of this system is that it places and keeps boys in a condition in which there is little opportunity of doing wrong. Their time is completely occupied: their attention is constantly fixed: they are never idle: they never deviate from a regular and steady course: whence the habit is formed of doing everything in its proper time and place. If the temptation to yield to bodily listlessness and mental dissipation occur, they are immediately roused to exertion by the active spirits around them, and compelled to put forth their strength, in order to keep pace with companions, by whom they feel it would be an intolerable disgrace to be outstripped. This practical moral lesson is repeated every day and every hour. The mind is induced to postpone its gratification as often as its temptation to yield to it recurs, and is stimulated to the steady performance of its duty (1 (1824), p. 74).

The *Westminster Review* was as opposed as evangelical journals to any activity likely to distract either mind or body from this performance of duty. 'The proper business of every man at every hour is to know as much as he can of political economy', a reviewer declared, while another insisted that self-interested pursuit of wealth was 'the greatest source of moral improvement' for the 'mass of mankind' (17 (1832), p. 1; 8 (1827), p. 186). Although the journal did review novels and plays (even at times sympathetically), it was during its first ten years as suspicious of imagination as the *Christian Observer*, which allowed no reviews of literature at all. The ultimate lesson of all fairy tales, superstitions and fictions, a *Westminster* reviewer insisted, was that 'all credit given to untruth, directly or indirectly, leads to misery' (14 (1833), p. 88). The first issue warned that 'exclusive culture of the faculty of imagination has but too strong a tendency to impair the powers of judgement', while, a few months later, another reviewer expressed even less patience: 'In sober and utilitarian sadness, we should be extremely glad to be informed, how the universal pursuit of literature and poetry, poetry and literature, is to conduce towards cotton-spinning ... Literature is a seducer; we had almost said a harlot' (1 (1824), p. 18; 4 (1825), p. 166).

Dickens's overt warning that, 'A country full of dismal little old men and women who had never played would be in a mighty bad way indeed' is well known,[4] but equally, all his novels should be understood as existing in a zone of polemical dialogization with the oppressive seriousness of this reactionary dominant culture. Moreover, within the early work, a speech image is constructed from the discourse of a series of characters which materializes a coherent strategy of resistance against forms of interpellation constituting subjects solely to work, obey, and confess. These fictional characters, who make a large contribution to the sparkling comic vitality of the early novels, are presented as wholly shaped by the marginalized culture of city streets. Their character discourse makes concrete the always subversive, parodic point of view of the common people, and the strategies deployed in their speech are the traditional ones of laughter and mockery. What these characters' language asserts is not any overt political programme, but a set of oppositional values; a subversive, nonhegemonic view of human life which challenges the hegemonic validity of dominant culture. The representation of characters like the red cabdriver in *Sketches by Boz*, the Artful Dodger and Charley Bates in *Oliver Twist*, Quilp's boy in *Old Curiosity Shop*, Young Bailey in *Martin Chuzzlewit*, and most fully developed of all, Sam and Tony Weller in *Pickwick Papers*, grows out of the actual language and materiality of London streets. The only other comparable source is Henry Mayhew's *London Labour and London Poor* whose pages provide ample guarantee of the historical basis of Dickens's street characters.

Pickwick Papers opens with parody of many forms of dominant discourse: of Parliamentary oratory and reports, of scientific investigations, of pious biographies, and of high-toned literature. However, the language of that first chapter is heavy and unfocussed. This is because the parodies do not imply clearly enough any alternative perspective against which their official voices are dialogized. The framing 'editorial' narrative is as much an object of parody as is the pompous language of the Pickwickians.

However, in Chapter Two another parodist steps forward, and this time the target is clearly defined against a fully realized alternative point of view. The presentation of the cab-driver's ironic send-up of Pickwick's scientific investigation into the tenacity of life in cab horses is a comic deflation of Pickwick, perceived from below as meddling authority. That this kind of response is an expression of a shared class attitude is signified in the representation of the cabman's confident appeal to the crowd which gathers instantly on the street, and in its vociferous support for him. However, almost equal to the urge to resist and mock Pickwick as officialdom, is the obvious zest with which the cabman enters into the drama of the situation. He not only appeals to the crowd, he performs for it with theatrical flourish, 'sparring away like clockwork', dashing his hat upon the ground, and dancing from the road to the pavement in a dizzying assault upon all four Pickwickians at once (9). Articulated in this small initial incident are the three essential qualities inhering in the marginal, nonhegemonic culture of the streets: an ironic impulse to deflate pomposity and officialdom, a cynical parodist's view of the discourse of those so perceived, enjoined with a physical zest which frequently expands into a theatrical performance of self as a spectacle to be enjoyed and shared by all participants in any occasion that offers.

These are precisely the qualities which characterize the speech image constructed by the discourse of Sam Weller as represented in his first encounter with Pickwick's solicitor, Mr Perker, at the White Hart Inn. Mr Perker's opening words are disarmingly encouraging: ' "My friend," said the thin gentleman'. But to be named is to be controlled, and Sam is not to be so easily interpellated into the role of obliging confident. ' "You're one o' the adwice gratis order," thought Sam, "or you wouldn't be so werry fond o' me all at once" ' (141). That alert suspicion of language images the cynical shrewdness developed in those whose precarious existence depends upon quickness of wit. The unworldly Mr Pickwick is presented as surprisingly shrewd when he sums up his prospective servant as possessing 'considerable knowledge of the world, and a great deal of sharpness' (171). 'Sharpness' is the term which most aptly describes those, like Sam Weller, shaped by the life of the streets, and it is the quality on which they most pride themselves. Tony Weller is represented as telling Mr Pickwick: 'I took a great deal o'pains with [Sam's] eddication, Sir; let him run in the streets when he was wery young, and shift for his-self. It's the only way to make a boy sharp, Sir' (298).

Henry Mayhew corroborated this judgement. Of the London street urchins, he wrote, 'The education of these children is such as only the streets afford; and the streets teach them for the most part – and in greater or lesser degrees – acuteness – a precocious acuteness'.[5] One of Mayhew's informants describes well how this 'acuteness' is expressed frequently in mockery of authority:

These young ones are as sharp as terriers, and learns every dodge of business in less of half of no time. There's one I knows about three foot high, that's up to the business as clever as a man of thirty. Though he's only twelve years old he'll chaff down a peeler so uncommon severe, that the only way to stop him is to take him in charge (I.35).

This is exactly the kind of 'precocious self-possession' represented in the character of Young Bailey, who, although 'an undersized boy ... yet he winked the winks, and thought the thoughts, and did the deeds, and said the sayings, of an ancient man' (420). Likewise the Artful Dodger is 'as dirty a juvenile as one could wish to see; but he had about him all the airs and manners of a man' (46). The sharpness of such characters, up to every dodge of business and full of ironic 'chaff', was as much a source of class pride as of personal esteem. The reflected rays of a sharp character's glory were felt by the working-class poor to increase their status generally. Mayhew admitted that even to boys from respectable working-class homes, 'the young street ruffian is a hero' (I.468). This importance attached to a reputation for sharpness is given expression in Tony Weller's indignation at Sam for allowing Job Trotter to fool him: 'Ought to ha' know'd better! why, I know a young 'un as hasn't had half nor quarter your eddication – as hasn't slept about the markets, no, not six months – who'd ha' scorned to be let in, in such a vay: scorned it, Sammy' (344–5). A similar sense of outrage is expressed when Charley Bates hears that the Artful Dodger is to be tried ingloriously on a petty charge.

'Sharpness' can best be defined as ironic knowingness, and, especially as imaged in the language of Sam Weller, this is manifest in a deeply cynical attitude towards the discourse of others. Mikhail Bakhtin claims that the traditional parodic-travestying forms of popular language function to break the grip of hegemonic discourse, since within parody two language images are brought into dialogic relation and the claims of each made relative against the ideological perspective of the other.[6] In view of this, it is not surprising that Sam Weller's cynical view of language is represented in the constant tendency of his discourse towards the dialogic and parodic. This is most clearly revealed in the structure of the Wellerisms. Almost uniformly these are of a hybrid construction in which the first half parodies a typical form of genteel dominant discourse, only to undercut its pretensions in the second half of the sentence by fusing it with an alternative, incongruous point of view. Thus a claim to rational authority in 'That's what I call a self-evident proposition' is rendered ludicrous when conjoined with 'as the dog's-meat man said when the housemaid told him he warn't a gentleman' (328). Appeal to natural necessity is mocked in 'I only assisted natur, Ma'am; as the doctor said to the boy's mother, arter he's bled him to death.', and the emptiness of much genteel urbanity exposed in 'Wery sorry to 'casion any personal inconwenience Ma'am; as the house breaker said to the old lady as he put her on the fire' (758, 394). In these last two examples the dialogized hybridization is further intensified as the lower-class form of pronunciation ironically undermines the elevated form of expression even while it is being uttered. In this way the frequent Wellerisms provide a parodic subversion throughout the novel of the claims to truth of any unitary form of language.

Little wonder then, that Sam is never presented as prisoner of another's discourse. Just as he sidesteps Mr Perker's urbane inter-pellation at the White Hart, so too, he is shown as immune to the legal mystifications of Dodson and Fogg, the verbal bullying of Serjeant Buzfuz, the sham ferocity of Mr Dowler, and the hypocritical piety of Mrs Weller and Mr Stiggins. The marginalized, parodic viewpoint constructed by Sam's character discourse is neatly demonstrated in his confident expectation of injustice from the law ('There ain't a magistrate going, as don't commit himself twice as often as he commits other people' (372)) in comparison to the sense of outrage in Pickwick's language when his trial betrays his unquestioned belief in the rightness of such institutions.

Parody strips away pretension to 'truth' and authority. However, language can also be used more creatively to deflate any person or thing seen as threatening by those without wealth or social standing to protect self-esteem. For centuries the poor invented nicknames to mock adversity which would otherwise degrade the value of their lives. Trouble cannot be avoided, but it can be transformed by laughter – hence the black jokes which characterize all folk humour. More than half the total of the Wellerisms have death as their subject. While harsh reality is left unsoftened by 'There's nothin' so refreshin' as sleep, Sir, as the servant-girl said afore she drunk the egg-cup full o' laudanum', the power of the harshness is snubbed by the humour (233). In the same spirit, Sam's discourse transforms the hardships of early years sleeping rough into playing 'leapfrog' with life's troubles (231), whilst the language of Charley Bates, in *Oliver Twist*, minimizes fear of the gallows with jokes about being 'scragged' (118). Language is used in a similar way to control the impositions of people who make any claim to authority. Sam is represented as brilliantly inventive of ironic nicknames: 'old Strike-a-light', 'Blazes', 'young dropsy', 'young brockiley sprout' are but a few of the names by which he denies any undue claims to dignity in those he meets.

At times the urge to ridicule is pursued with such creative energy that it expands into a self-sustaining theatrical performance. The earliest representation of this is of the last cabdriver, in *Sketches by Boz*, appearing before the magistrates at the Mansion House and turning the case against himself into subversive comedy. The Dodger, at his trial, is depicted also as capturing the proceedings with a bravura parodic performance of the dominant discourses of Law, the City, Parliament, and Society. This whole episode is presented from a marginalized class perspective: the Dodger's performance delights the crowd by exposing the inequality of Victorian justice, and, while not saving the Dodger from its power to deport, lifts him beyond humiliation and the repressive imposition of guilt. Indeed, it is the Dodger, like Sam Weller, who accuses – 'this ain't the shop for justice' – and concludes by sentencing himself out of the presence of a degraded law:

> 'I wouldn't go free, now, if you was to fall down on your knees and ask me. Here, carry me off to prison! Take me away!'
> With these last words, the Dodger suffered himself to be led off by the collar; threatening, till he got into the yard to make a parliamentary business of it; and then grinning in the officer's face with great glee and self-approval (300).

An equally exuberant representation of parodic performance is Trabb's boy, a late reappearance of the street urchin type, who mocks Pip's upstart pride by swaggering along the street in a carpet bag, disdainfully declaiming, 'Don't know yah, don't know yah, pon my soul don't know yah!' (232).

Within *Pickwick Papers*, the zone of sharpest dialogic opposition is that between Sam Weller's character discourse and the language of most of the inserted tales. This marks the beginning of that conflict felt within subsequent texts between an overt moral plot and the social plot of the subtext. All of the non-comic tales tend towards the heavy seriousness of tone which characterizes hegemonic discourse. Heteroglossia with its multiplicity of conflicting viewpoints is firmly exluded; the narrator and the various characters all speak with the same unitary voice. Without exception the narrative structure of these tales functions to unfold a causal moral logic solemnly illustrative of the consequences of wrongdoing. In other words, they are strikingly similar in form to the countless moral biographies which fill the pages of the evangelical journals, demonstrating the inexorable causal chain running from youthful high spirits to profligacy, loss of wealth and respectability, and culminating reliably in remorse and despair. The clichèd, melodramatic language of the non-comic inserted tales in *Pickwick* moves along a vertical axis of metaphoric condensation to valorize apparently universal 'laws' of nature and timeless ideals. The patient suffering mother in 'The Convict's Return', for example, like the wife in 'The Stroller's Tale', symbolizes virtuous Woman generally, and beyond that the Christian values of meekness and endurance.

The Sam Weller tales are resolutely heteroglot, composed almost entirely of dialogue. They therefore embrace plurality of viewpoint in contrast to the claims of necessary truth implied in the unitary tone of the moral tales. The structuring principle of Sam's narrative language is essentially metonymic; subordinating conjunctions figure very rarely, the simple clauses being loosely linked by a dash or 'and'. This metonymic freedom from syntactic hierarchy dialogically subverts the insistent moral and 'scientific' causal logic stressed by hegemonic discourse in its ideological narratives. The metonymic openness of Sam Weller's language allows for the contingent, comic association of incongruous incidents and things. In his stories, Sam asserts a necessary causal relationship between such absurdly unrelated things as poverty and oysters, postboys and donkeys, death from muffins, and a fit of insanity causing its victim to 'rashly convert his-self into sassages' (465). Causal significance is mocked also by eccentric attention to details quite inconsequential to narrative logic, as in the tale of the man who dies of eating muffins. There, the narrative moves with metonymic fluidity from the man falling ill, the doctor being called, to a wholly unrelated description of the adaptation of the doctor's coach so that he can descend without the assistance of his coachman who has no trousers to match the livery of his coat.

Utilitarian insistence that facts are incontestable, that there is a necessary connection between cause and effect, and evangelical insistence upon the exact correspondence between signifier and signified – outward appearance a reliable sign of inner grace – are alike undermined by the ludic associations and contingent logic of the Sam Weller narratives. In the world they construct, the relationship between signifier and signified is arbitrary indeed, and the signifier moves with metonymic freedom:

'They're all made o' them noble animals,' says he, a pointin' to a wery nice little tabby kitten, 'and I seasons 'em for beefsteak, weal, or kidney, 'cordin to the demand; and more than that,' says he, 'I can make a weal a beefsteak, or a beef-steak a kidney, or any one on 'em a mutton, at a minute's notice, just as the market changes, and appetites wary' (278).

In all these ways the language of the streets imaged in Dickens's early novels, dialogizes subversively with dominant discourse inside and outside the texts. However, the role of the street characters who materialize this nonhegemonic point of view is not only a negative one. Their presentation also gives concrete expression to a positive and imaginative view of human existence in opposition to the gloomy, life-repressing outlook of Utilitarians and evangelicals and their manipulation of failure, sin, and guilt as means of social control.

In sharp contrast to the Utilitarian views of existence as a competitive struggle between individuals, or the evangelical vision of life as 'a warfare and a pilgrimage', the street characters in Dickens's texts celebrate the process of living in a spirit of carnival and laughter. Celebration of life, including the life of the body, is expressed in pleasure in dress: for street characters clothes are an affirmative language. Mayhew wrote of a coster lad he interviewed, that 'he was dressed in all the slang beauty of his class, with bright red handkerchief and unexceptional boots' (I.39). The last cabdriver, in *Sketches*, is depicted with a similar love of colour – his cab being 'gorgeously painted' and his neck 'usually garnished with a bright yellow handkerchief' (142). Sam Weller is introduced into the text wearing 'a bright red handkerchief . . . wound in a very loose and unstudied style round his neck, and an old white hat was carelessly thrown on one side of his head' (137). The Artful Dodger, too, is represented as carrying his hat at a defiant angle, so far to the back of his head that it was in constant danger of falling off (46). Along with this flippant positioning of headgear, goes a propensity for unbuttoned jackets, loose cravats and scarves, all suggestive of a responsive openness to life, very different from those starched and tightly buttoned characters like Dombey, Podsnap, and Headstone; repressed and repressing. There is a metonymic expansiveness to the description of Tony Weller which conveys a whole-hearted embrace of life. His crimson travelling shawl merges into his chin in 'imperceptible gradations' while his face 'had expanded under the influence of good living . . . and its bold fleshy curves had ... far extended beyond the limits originally assigned them' (343).

Typically this description introduces Tony Weller at meat and drink, exhibiting a Rabelasian appetite, and celebrating the pleasures of the flesh with gusto. The impression conveyed is not one of gluttony, but it is equally far removed from any utilitarian sense of merely providing the nourishment to sustain life. As in Charley Bates's eulogy for the rabbit pie he brings to an impoverished Bill Sikes (in which we can clearly discern the elaborate praises of city street vendors), pleasure in abundance, as expressed by working-class characters, is rooted in the experience of need: ' "Sitch a rabbit pie, Bill," exclaimed that young gentleman, disclosing to view a huge pasty; "sitch delicate creeturs, with sitch tender limbs, Bill, that the wery bones melt in your mouth, and there's no occasion to pick 'em" ' (259). Outside Dickens's texts, Utilitarians argued the mistaken kindness of supplementing the starvation diet of the poor, and evangelicals saw every glass of beer swallowed by working men as further proof of their degeneracy. Inside his texts, genteel characters are frequently represented as pretending to eat little, ashamed to acknowledge physical needs shared with common people. By contrast, in the representation of characters like Sam and Tony Weller, eating and drinking are associated always with the values of communality: with festive good humour, talk, laughter, and companionship. Food and fellowship become almost organically linked, as in the typical 'feast' presided over by Sam in the kitchen of Mr Nupkins, where 'the beer and the cold meat, and the laughter combined' in an atmosphere of 'jollity and conviviality' (385).

This sense of communality is in active opposition to a belief in self-interest as the mainspring motivating human action. The streets breed cynicism, but also an experience of shared hardship, encouraging an unsentimental but responsive fellowship with suffering. A young pickpocket told Mayhew, 'I would rather rob the rich than the poor; they miss it less' (I.411). The language of similar characters within Dickens's texts images this same mixture of realism and sympathy. Young Bailey is presented as unscandalized by Jonas Chuzzlewit's drunkenness, but indignant when he illtreats his wife. The Dodger spends his last money with grandiose flair, buying food for Oliver Twist who is starving: 'You want grub, and you shall have it. I'm at low-water-mark myself – only one bob and a magpie, but *as far as* it goes, I'll fork out and stump' (47). There is no cynicism, only sympathy in Sam Weller's description of the vagrants who sleep rough under

Waterloo Bridge: 'worn-out, starving, houseless creeturs as rolls themselves up in the dark corners o' them lonesome places' (231).

What the presentation of such characters asserts, through their convivial laughter, their sympathy, their nonhegemonic speech, and their imaginative exuberance, is that life is not warfare against sin, nor is it only competitive struggle; life, including its many hardships, can be embraced and enhanced in a spirit of play — Sam Weller's transforming image of leapfrog with life. Material possessions are few, but life offers a contingent, inconsequential abundance of everyday happenings and absurdities, and even more, the inventive resources of people's linguistic and performative capacities, all of which can be playfully and comically celebrated. Amidst the daily drudgery at Todgers, Young Bailey is presented as sustaining a sense of comic superfluity, as when, laying the supper table for the Miss Pecksniffs, he entertains them 'by thrusting the lighted candle into his mouth, and exhibiting his face in a state of transparency' (143). Those without wealth or status to embellish the image of their lives become imaginatively adept at exploiting language, gesture, and common reality to transform, with a sense of ceremony, existences which would otherwise be overwhelmed by necessity and utility.

Even a cursory glance through the pages of *London Labour* confirms the material basis of this desire to transform everyday incidents with comic performance and ceremony. Almost every person that Mayhew interviews is an instinctive comedian or story-teller. Louis James, in *Print and the People 1819–1851* also writes of the 'working-class love of ritual' in which 'daily transactions and moments such as apprenticeship or a new job, all had their little ceremonials usually accompanied by a drink'.[7] Just such a transaction is represented in *Pickwick Papers*, when Tony Weller's fellow coachmen, each sporting a ceremonial dahlia, congregate to celebrate his inheritance of his late wife's property. They are presented as enhancing this occasion by an impressively dramatic ritual:

'Hold hard there,' interposed the mottled-faced gentleman, with sudden energy, 'your eyes on me, gen'lm'n.'

Saying this, the mottled-faced gentleman rose, as did the other gentlemen. The mottled-faced gentleman reviewed the company, and slowly raised his hand, upon which every man (including him of the mottled countenance) drew a long breath, and lifted his tumbler to his lips. In one instant the mottled-faced gentleman depressed his hand again, and every glass was set down empty. It is impossible to describe the thrilling effect produced by this striking ceremony; at once dignified, solemn, and impressive, it combined every element of grandeur (853).

There is a firm distinction to be drawn between the implications of this episode and the representation of the 'swarry' Sam attends in the company of the servants at Bath. Whereas the coachmen are shown performing for themselves, to enhance the memorability of a shared moment uniting all the participants in equal dignity, the text carefully conveys a sense with the servants that they are looking over their shoulders to see how well they are impressing the rest of the world. The coachmen's ceremony is presented as self-generated, while the servants engage in a slavish imitation of their perceived superiors. This contrast constructs fictional images of the historical transition from a stable, traditional world to one of individualist mobility. *Pickwick Papers* represents Tony Weller and his fellow coachmen as deriving their sense of identity and worth from the time-honoured mystique of their craft community. The servants are shown as men of a modern individualistic world, engaged in a competitive struggle for status, where all must assert their own value against all others. What the text reveals, but what the servants fail to perceive, is that despite claims of equality with their employers, the very desire to conform to an imaginary ideal of gentility mirrors back their own sense of lack. Hence the need to bridge the gap between self and ego-ideal with a vicarious experience of superiority obtained by bullying the greengrocer paid to wait upon them. This competitive, isolating struggle for personal predominance – social and moral – typifies relations in a society where status and identity are conceived in terms of comparative worth.

In sharp contrast to this individualistic self-assertion, the performances of self, as elaborated in the presentation of characters like Sam Weller, the Dodger, Pickwick's cabman, or Young Bailey, are defined by a participatory playfulness which recruits any audience into the act. The theatricality of the servants represents the closure of conformity with a set ideal; the theatricality of the street characters is depicted as a creative process – they make and remake themselves. For them, existence is continuous transformation in time and place as they seize upon and respond opportunistically to every contingent situation, exploiting its potential for playful inventiveness. This form of playful self-making is, needless to say, in complete defiance of those divine, natural and economic 'laws' which, all the hegemonic voices of Victorian England insisted, wholly determine human life. Neither is it compatible with any essentialist unitary account of subjectivity. These performances of self are not the outward manifestation of some inner essential being. These street characters are what they act at that moment – they are their surfaces – an embodiment of the supremacy of the signifier.

As this implies, a more helpful model of self is the Lacanian one of decentred displacement along a chain of metonymic association. However, this is not displacement in pursuit of some desired Absolute Subject, in which the will to conform to the ideal image must necessarily mirror back a sense of lack and inadequacy. These characters are presented as creating an image of self-in-process through a freewheeling imaginative response to anything a given situation suggests. The most stunning and comic representation of this occurs in *Martin Chuzzlewit* when Young Bailey notices Poll Sweedlepipe's barber's equipment. This sparks off the notion of a shave – to Poll's horror since Bailey's youthful chin is as 'smooth as a new-laid egg'. However, such is the panache of Bailey's performance that 'evidence of sight and touch became as nothing' to the bewildered Poll, and encouraged by Bailey to 'Go in and win', he applies lather bountifully (458). As this is scraped off, Bailey is represented as capping the performance by murmuring regretfully at non-existent bristles, 'Reether redder than I could wish, Poll' (461).

While such cavalier disregard of referents in favour of the signifier accords with Lacanian assertions, it must be noted that Dickens's representation of the decentred subject, as it is materialized in these marginal characters of the city streets, is inherently optimistic.[8] A decentred subject can espouse the fluid displacements of the metonymic chain to playfully create as many selves as possible, just as these are suggested by free association with the material world. Such a model of active, theatrical self-making, combined with a parodic distrust of language, offers a strategy of escape from the imposition of an imprisoning social self bound in by the internalized repressions of guilt and inadequacy. Such were the enclosing models offered by all the voices of dominant discourse with their debarring of imagination and their insistence on the inevitable causal relationship between industrious effort and wealth, gentility and spiritual grace, poverty and improvidence.

The free play with signifiers in the theatrical constitution of self-images is only possible as co-operative, communal activity. As with all language, signification is achieved, not from any necessary relation between signifier and signified, but through common consent and recognition. Unlike subjective conceptions of self, this public constitution of self aims at something beyond individual fulfilment. The theatricality, the wit, and the audacity are intended to irradiate the whole people, the whole class, with glamour; to liberate them all from the grip of utility and necessity in a spirit of play and comic freedom. The fullest materialization of this is the description of the feast which takes place at Todgers, presided over by Young Bailey. The language of the text foregrounds abundance and superfluity: the table groans 'beneath the weight ... of boiled beef, roast veal, bacon pies ... heavy vegetables ... bottles of stout, bottles of wine, bottles of ale; and divers other strong drinks, native and foreign' (147). There are 'quarts of almonds; dozens of oranges; pounds of raisins; stacks of biffins' (148). There is yet more wine and a large bowl of punch, but flowing even more freely is the shared enthusiasm and conviviality. In this atmosphere, each lodger performs an image of self, not for individualistic elevation, but to enhance a communal sense of occasion and festival: 'Every man comes out freely in his own character. The gentleman of a theatrical turn recites. The vocal gentleman regales them with a song. Gander leaves the Gander of all former feasts whole leagues behind' (149).

'The feast,' writes Bakhtin, 'has no utilitarian connotations ... On the contrary, the feast means liberation from all that is utilitarian, practical. It is a temporary transfer to the utopian world.'[9] In such scenes and in such characters as here described, Dickens's texts construct a transformative utopian vision; one which has a strength and vitality unavailable elsewhere in English fiction. The strength comes from the sureness of the presentation, based in the material reality of an actual culture and discourse – the working-class life and language of city streets. It is vital because, unlike many utopias, it is not shut off from temporality. Indeed, time and place constitute it. The process of continuous displacement along a metonymic chain of contingent association opposes hierarchical values and timeless verities, transforming the activities of everyday living into playful art. The realm of freedom springs from and is sustained by the realm of necessity.

Notes

1. *Methodist Magazine* (1831), p. 476. Subsequent references will be indicated in the text. While many Methodists, especially those who were working class, did not identify with the prevailing political discourse, *Methodist Magazine*, with its huge circulation, was undoubtedly the voice of the increasingly dominant majority who did espouse and actively support the political and social Establishment.

2. 'Chartism' in *Selected Essays* (1972), p. 177.
3. Quoted in Michael Rose, *The Relief of Poverty 1834–1914* (1972), p. 17.
4. *Speeches*, p. 272.
5. *London Labour and London Poor*, 4 vols (New York, 1968), I, 24. Subsequent references will be indicated in the text.
6. *The Dialogic Imagination*, pp. 74–6.
7. *Print and the People 1819–1851* (1976), p. 65.
8. There is no facile optimism, however. Another series of characters, including Nancy in *Oliver Twist*, Jo in *Bleak House*, Magwitch in *Great Expectations*, points out the fate on the streets awaiting those who are not sharp.
9. *Rabelais and His World*, translated by Helene Iswolsky (Cambridge, Massachusetts, 1968), p. 276.

2

Martin Chuzzlewit: Anger

Dickens's novels are discursive events, reactive and dialogic. Words in his texts are saturated with the shifting power struggles active within the heteroglossia of the era. The early 1840s, which produced *Martin Chuzzlewit*, were years of particularly marked social tension, the deepest levels of which never quite reached the surface of public discussion. The topic of emigration within dominant discourse – as within *Chuzzlewit* – served as a kind of nodal point knotting together a cluster of anxieties about economic competition, violent social energies, over-population, and even the position of women. *The Times* ran many hostile leading articles on the subject of emigration, and described its columns as 'teeming' with accounts of inhuman treatment to luckless emigrants (27 November 1841). The *Westminster Review* wrote more sympathetically that 'the great activity of colonization is among the most conspicuous features of the times' (35 (1841), 132). The words 'teeming' and 'activity' in those quotations form part of an associative chain of deeply ambivalent words and images which recurred continually throughout dominant discourse, conveying a sense of struggle for survival in all aspects of social life. This network of ambivalence inscribed an ideological conflict around the oppositions of energy and restraint, life and death. The multiple engagement of the text of *Martin Chuzzlewit* in this conflict makes it the novel by Dickens with the most immediate affinity to Britain in the 1980s. This is particularly striking in the pervasive parallels the novel draws between American and English cultural and economic development. In both countries and in both eras the pursuit and accumulation of wealth becomes the valorized object of all human desire – a universal 'golden calf' into which all 'cares, hopes, joys, affections, virtues, and associations [are] to be melted down' (273).

The years from the mid-1830s to the mid-1840s could be termed a decade of triumph for the competitive individualistic ideal. As early as 1826 the *Westminster Review* was able to claim that the 'spirit of speculation' was widely accepted and that government was 'willing to give the enterprise of the community its full play, and to trust individuals with the superintendance of their own interests' (5 (1826), 127–8). The necessity of freedom from all restraint, the unmitigated virtue of unleashed energies in the pursuit of wealth, and the mechanism of unbridled self-interest as the sole means of general good became almost unchallenged themes of dominant discourse. A book called *Progress of the Nation*, written in 1847 by a statistician at the Board of Trade, boasted that the economic agents of material progress were 'working with incessant and increasing energy' so that the financial success of the country had 'made the greatest advances in civilization' ever recorded.[1] This claim of an economic miracle was not much exaggerated; the gross national income of Great Britain rose from £340 millions in 1831 to over £523 millions in 1851.

However, this period of capitalist triumph was not a smooth upward surge of economic expansion for all, but a familiar pattern of boom and depression. For vast numbers of individuals it was experienced as dislocation, insecurity, and, frequently, extreme privation. These inevitable consequences of a time of rapid social transition were made more severe by the imposition of a harsher system of welfare in the form of the New Poor Laws, introduced to eradicate dependency and to stimulate enterprise. The prolonged financial slump of 1837–42, bringing with it destitution on a vast scale, was a major factor in the accelerating emigration figures. The unleashing of entrepreneurial energies, welcomed by some, brought to others the experience of unleashed hardship, and a loss of connection with older securities and ties of home.

In the early stages of industrialization the typical entrepreneur was a merchant-employer, who individually owned and controlled his whole business enterprise, frequently living upon the premises. However, the late 1830s and early 1840s marked the moment of transition from this type of individual ownership towards corporate capitalism.[2] The campaign against all forms of commercial restraint led to the deregulation of banking and company law by Parliamentary Acts in 1826, 1837, and 1844. This last Act legalized the formation of joint-stock companies and in the ensuing years the number of such enterprises, depending upon multiple speculative investment, increased rapidly. In *Martin Chuzzlewit*, the replacement of 'the old-established firm of Antony Chuzzlewit and Son, Manchester Warehousemen' by the 'Anglo-Bengalee Disinterested Loan and Life Assurance Company' represents precisely this transition of capitalist mode, with the concomitant shift of economic power away from an industrial base to the commerial City of London.[3] Far from following in the wake of social movement, Dickens's text registers an initial moment of historical change. In 1844, as *Martin Chuzzlewit* was published, speculative activity in railways and other commercial projects was about to explode. Although a modern American historian has written optimistically of this expansion of joint-stock companies as the means of spreading entrepreneurial enthusiasm and of familiarizing more people with the idea of speculative investment,[4] the increase undoubtedly added to the sense of financial insecurity of the period. Looking back on this burst of new commercial activity the *Methodist Magazine* wrote: 'A few years ago our bountiful Lord gave us much commercial success. ... [But] did not thousands of Christian people turn into money seeking courses, which were commercially of most anxious hazard ... Did not thousands who might have had enough of earthly good ... so pant for wealth, and wealth not gained by patient industry, but by adroit speculation' (1849, p. 275).

The one word which most powerfully condensed and contained the whole complex of ambivalence aroused by the changed climate of competitive capitalism was 'struggle'. The *Christian Observer* focussed upon the use of this word by a well-known American writer, a Miss Sedgewick, then on a much-publicized tour of England. Miss Sedgewick was surprised by the numbers of people thronging the streets 'vigorously competing for any casual employment'. She was told by them that they were 'struggling for bread' (1842, pp. 700–1). Miss Sedgewick, very like one of Dickens's boastful American characters, responded to this by asserting that such 'struggle' for existence was unknown in her country.[5] The *Westminster Review* also made use of this word to explain why emigration was spreading to people of the middle and upper classes. At the present time, it claimed, all but the very wealthy were 'engaged in a perpetual struggle to maintain themselves in the position in society to which they belong, but from which numbers are continually thrust by the superior energies of their fellows. That there is not room for all is obvious to all, and this necessarily induces a struggle of painful intensity' (35 (1841), 134). Those involved in this 'struggle' to maintain position were termed 'young men of the uneasy class', a description which seems to fit young Martin Chuzzlewit most aptly. His grandfather's description of the competitive thrust for survival is more emotive than that of the *Westminster Review*: 'Brother against brother, child against parent, friends treading on the faces of friends' (39).

The context of the *Christian Observer*'s emphasis on the word 'struggle' was an article on Chartism and recent rioting. The decade of triumphant capitalist enterprise was also characterized by intense political struggle and social unrest among the working class. This was the fracture point of contradiction within the dominant ideology of competitive individualism. Demands for greater freedom and the pursuit of self-improvement were unacceptable when articulated on behalf of the working class in the Chartists' ten points. The restless questing energy acclaimed by middle-class advocates of the competitive spirit assumed a dangerous form when it surfaced in working-class protest and anger. The discourse articulating this fear of working-class revolt was structured upon that ambivalent opposition of freedom and restraint. Imminent revolution was consistently described as an explosion of pent-up energy, but energy which had become diseased and putrescent from containment and restraint. Drawing parallels between Chartism and the French Revolution, the *Westminster Review* described the latter as 'the last stage in a process of social decomposition – the violent escape of pent-up gasses from a corrupted mass' (36 (1841), 154). The *Methodist Magazine* echoed this lurid imagery, warning against 'a fatal issue of the corrupt fermentation ... going on in the recesses of our body politic' (1843, p. 817). This ambiguous fusion of energy with disease led to confusion in the *Christian Observer*. Referring to 'revolutionary' occurrences within the country, it concluded 'we are standing upon a volcano ... ready to burst out'. However, the writer continued with an interesting analogy which unwittingly undercut his previous warning:

> Look, says the geologist, at those mountains and valleys ... processes are going on by which they are tending to one dead level, which they must reach, unless a volcano, or earthquake, ... creates new variety of surface ... unless some counteracting agency should take place, the whole world will become a bed of mud, levelled to the uniformity of surface by the waters which invest it. And thus is modern society tending to democracy. In the United States of America the process is nearly complete (1840, pp. 124–5).

Thus the volcanic energy of Chartism, according to the reviewer, would save England from the mud of democracy which was the goal of its struggle!

The vision of America projected by the text of *Martin Chuzzlewit*, especially in the Eden section, is strikingly like that of the *Christian*

Observer – it is a bed of mud. Furthermore, the language of the novel draws pervasively upon the lurid imagery used within dominant discourse. Eden is a 'hideous swamp' with trees like 'huge weeds begotten of slime' and a 'foetid vapour'. The proper division and order of things has been lost in a primeval decomposition: nothing is 'divisible into their separate kinds ... [all is] a jungle deep and dark, with neither earth nor water at its roots, but putrid matter, formed of the pulpy offal of the two, and of their own corruption' (377, 379). The citizens of America are represented to be as indistinguishable and weed-like as the vegetation.

However, Chevy Slyme is an English weed. And it is from England as a 'cramped prison' with 'Want, colder than Charity, shivering at the street corners' that energy bursts free (245). Wind and clouds rush out like 'pent-up gasses' into the unrestricted space of ocean: 'Here in the fury of their unchecked liberty, they storm and buffet with each other, until the sea, lashed into passion like their own, leaps up, in ravings mightier than theirs, and the whole scene is madness' (245). The text here enacts a double displacement. The lashed-up elemental passions are a projection of violent human passions the hero will encounter in America, but the imagery points backwards and beyond the text to the domestic 'madness' of rioting and violence brought about by the 'cramped prison' of poverty and Poor Law charity in England. Less ambiguously presented is old Martin's desire to overthrow the injustice of Pecksniff – a passion intensified by 'forced and unnaturally nurtured energy consequent upon ... long suppression' (790).

Yet another form of competitive struggle interconnected with the fear of unleashed political anger, deepening the ideological ambivalence centred upon imagery of energy and restraint. The census of 1841 revealed a population increase of well over two million since 1831. Malthusian fears of population excess seemed about to be fulfilled; the discourse of the time conveyed a sense of 'teeming' numbers struggling for survival and exacerbating social tensions. The official voices in early Victorian England felt bound to affirm this increase a blessing of Providence, yet all too obviously the blessing of abundant life was toppling over into its opposite – the curse of death and disease. Even the *Christian Observer* warned, 'rapid multiplication will be checked by poverty and disease; the people will be sickly' (1842, p. 380). The cause of this perversion of Providence was found in the unruly 'passions' of the 'numerous classes' leading them into reckless parenthood. Again it seemed that the thrusting energies driving middle-class entrepreneurial expansion assumed, in the working class, a dangerously distorted form. Lack of restraint by the poor, declared the *Westminster Review*, was transforming the nation into 'a squalid and debilitated race, who inherit from their parents disease, sometimes deformity, often vice, always beggary' (18 (1833), 391). Again, the text of *Chuzzlewit* displaces this social fear of an excessive life force degenerating into a deformed weed-like growth onto the emotive imagery of America, where 'trees had grown so thick and close that they shouldered one another out of their places, and the weakest, forced into shapes of strange distortion, languished like cripples. The best were stunted, from the pressure and want of room' (379).

This fear of a struggling conflict of energy, barely articulated, but pervasive in all the predominating themes of public discourse in the early 1840s, constructs the sense of a life force seized by its opposite and rechannelled into an impulse towards destruction and death. This evokes Freud's account of the struggle, within individuals and cultures, of the life and death instincts. The evolution of civilization, Freud writes, is in fact 'the struggle between Eros and Death, between the instinct of life and the instinct of destruction, as it works itself out in the human species'.[6] In this struggle both instincts fight to gain mastery of desire as the force driving all activity. Eros (the life or sexual instincts) functions in the service of society, combining individuals into 'families, then races, peoples and nations, into one great unity, the unity of mankind'.[7] The most obvious manifestations of the destructive instincts are aggression and sadism, whereby the death impulse is projected away from masochistic harm of self and out onto the object world. However, the destructive instincts can be modified and tamed so that they appear to serve the ends of Eros in exerting control over the material world and thus providing for the satisfaction of needs. In this form much of the apparent 'progress' of civilization may be, in fact, the sublimated work of the death instincts. However, there remains always a danger that these instincts will escape the restraining control of Eros and impel civilization towards death and destructiveness.[8]

As well as offering a means of more fully articulating the social fears submerged like a repressed unconscious within public discourse of the 1840s, Freud's speculations provide a useful conceptual framework within which to read *Martin Chuzzlewit* — itself part of the 1840s discourse. The sense of energy bursting out of control in the service of death is articulated almost explicitly in the description of the death of old Anthony Chuzzlewit: 'It was frightful to see how the principle of life, shut up within his withered frame, fought like a strong devil, mad to be released, and rent its ancient prison house' (306). In a similar way, the impulse of death imposes itself upon all character discourse like the return of a barely repressed obsession constantly forcing its way to the surface in words. Mark Tapley, for example, looks for work in a 'grave-digging way', and Pecksniff even invokes death in the pursuit of Eros: 'Has a voice from the grave no influence' (68, 151). Far from being a garden of Eden, individualistic culture on both sides of the Atlantic, as constructed by narrative and character discourse, belongs to a fallen world – Sairey's 'wale', and as she maintains, 'the consequence of sech a sitivation' is that death is the impulse behind all life. It is a repressed which only returns the more aggressively for restraint.

There is one more theme within 1840s public discourse which needs to be articulated in relation to *Martin Chuzzlewit*. In 1841 the *Westminster Review* pointed out that 'the situation of women is, at this moment, a matter of interest and discussion' and it went on to review some of the many books just published on this subject (35 (1841), 24). At a time of alarm over population excess, women inevitably became a focus of attention. Their capacity for restraint of sexual passion was regarded as more trustworthy than that of men. However, the role of women intersected yet more pervasively with social anxieties. Their political situation paralleled that of working-class men. Both groups were marginalized, and both were regarded as dangerously lacking rational judgement, requiring firm guidance from a patriarchal male as husband, father, or employer. The elaboration of the myth of a 'feminine' submissiveness and gentleness during these years of intense psychic anxiety over the need for competitive energy in the aggressive struggle to survive must be seen, therefore, as the social construction of an imaginary 'solution' or imaginary counterforce to fears and pressures which could not be avoided in the real world. Thus the ideological image of women as 'naturally' chaste and self-repressing projected a comforting model of social docility across the spectrum of anxiety – a denial of sexual and political discontent. The word 'passion', part of that network of ambivalence, revealed the interconnection of these concerns. It was used interchangeably to refer to dangerous political energy, to sexuality, and to expressions of anger – particularly in women; in this way it facilitated a continual blurring of distinctions across forbidden sexual and political boundaries. The dialogic engagement of *Chuzzlewit* is revealed by a recurrent return of the word 'passion' to its discourse.

However, in practice the extinction of passion was not always so 'naturally' effected and perhaps was not even totally desirable. One of the books on women discussed in the *Westminster Review* deplored the restrictive upbringing of girls which was making them too lacking in vitality to provide suitable wives for emigrants. Another reviewed book voiced more openly the fear that restraint could be destructive. Enforced spinsterhood led young women to grow 'thin, pale, listless, and cross, at last, if they do not go mad or die of consumption, seeking consolation in the belief of an approaching millenium' (35 (1841), 135). Barely articulated here is that recurring fear of the times that energies if repressed will turn masochistically upon themselves seeking death, or, more threateningly, explode outwards in the uncontrolled passions of sexuality, anger, or political unrest – desire for a millenium. Because of the parallel political marginalization of women and working-class men, any expression of rage or discontent in women was as severely censured as sexual misconduct.[9] While the myth of women's 'natural' chastity was elaborated to police women's sexual energies, the 'hystericization' of women constructed a discourse able to depoliticize their anger.

The seemingly apolitical text of *Martin Chuzzlewit* works to displace these interconnected conflicts into a fictional representation where they can interact dialogically without arousing alarm, and where imaginary 'solutions' to the ideological tensions can be offered through plot resolution, speech images, and character representation.[10] In addition, as already indicated, the text plays for safety by displacing many of the political anxieties onto the American episodes, whilst the language used continues to draw upon prevalent imagery within the dominant discourse of 1840s England.

American life is characterized in the text as a struggle for survival in a culture which sanctions unrestrained outbursts of individual aggressiveness. The 'bubbling passions' of destructive anger continually 'find vent' in murder or grievous harm (256). The rhetoric of individualistic freedom articulated by American discourse in the text offers an image of competitive energies out of control. In the language of many of the American characters represented, the death instincts are overt and markedly unrepressed. The freedom of self so vigorously proclaimed is materialized in the right to kill others. However, in the English section of the novel, the speech image constructed by Jonas Chuzzlewit's language represents a similarly unrestrained form of self-assertion. A barely repressed death impulse towards his father pushes continually into his discourse. As in America, this aggressive pursuit of self-interest is linked firmly to cultural values – specifically to the commercial sense of a competitive struggle for survival: ' "Do other men, for they would do you". That's the true business precept' he says (181). Anthony Chuzzlewit's discourse corroborates the shaping influence of commercial principles upon Jonas: 'I trained him. This is the heir of my upbringing ... he'll not squander my money' (180). Jonas's discourse, like that of the American characters, admits no restraint upon individualistic self-interest: 'You can't overdo taking care of yourself' (181). Furthermore, the aggressive self-assertion of his speech image takes material form in physical violence. The destructive energies in control of Jonas are linked implicitly to an impulse of sexual sadism. Freud considered this the most common manifestation of the death instincts gaining control of the sexual or life instincts. Jonas's attraction to Merry Chuzzlewit is represented as a desire to humiliate and subdue by physical brutality: 'As he made an angry motion with his hand, she shrunk down hastily. A suggestive action! Full of a cruel truth' (712). The destructive impulse of 'doing' others culminates in the murder of Tigg. The full irony involved in the representation of this is that by removing the last restraints upon the death instincts within himself in order to save self, Jonas actually 'does' for himself. After the murder he becomes 'not only fearful *for* himself, but *of* himself' (724).[11] Inevitably the end is violent self-destruction. In representing this the text brings together in a single image the interconnecting ideas of competitive struggle, greed, energy, and death. Jonas's dead hand clutches the poison bottle 'with that rigidity of grasp with which no living man, in the full strength and energy of life, can clutch a prize he has won' (790).

Tigg, the object of the destructive impulses in Jonas, is identified also with him. In the nightmare he is presented as having before he is murdered, Tigg's terror moves ambivalently between an inner and an external source of fear; the destructive instincts are represented as both within and without. The identity of the two characters is signified by the identity of their speech images. Tigg's individualistic business ethics echo those of Jonas; the Anglo-Bengalee Company is 'a capital concern ... in one sense ... the only important one ... which is number one' (428). Again the text drives home the cultural values implicit in this assertion; the word 'capital' is repeated five times within almost as many lines. However, Tigg represents the beginning of corporate capitalism. Whereas Jonas's aggression projects itself directly upon the external world, that of Tigg is mediated into multiple indirect channels. His victims are 'the multitude' in the 'crowded streets' who 'bring us their money in a hundred shapes and ways, force it upon us, trust us as if we were the Mint; yet know no more about us than ... of that crossing-sweeper at the corner' (444). This testimony to the spreading enthusiasm for speculative investment among ordinary people is greeted with approbation by Jonas as 'a capital notion'. Tigg, elaborating the diverse methods of obtaining such 'investment', readily admits that such 'very profitable' activity is 'capital fun' (445). The text is discreet in that it thus allows the discourse of disreputable characters to make these cynical disclosures about the way speculative capitalism often practices destructively upon the trusting and vulnerable – those ill-equipped in a competitive society.[12]

By contrast, in the American section diegetic commentary is indignant and explicit in linking speculation to fraud and the destruction of life: 'In commercial affairs he was a bold speculator. In plainer words, he had a most distinguished genius for swindling ... (entailing ruin, pestilence, and death on hundreds of families) ... This made him an admirable man of business' (268–9). Nearer home, Tigg asserts, 'There is nothing like building our fortunes on the weaknesses of mankind' (680). Diegetic comment does not endorse this as a general truth about English commercial practice. Nevertheless, the text significantly fails to offer any alternative image of corporate capitalism in England to that of the Anglo-Bengalee. A further implicit parallel between American and English economic culture is drawn in the selling techniques used on either side of the Atlantic. Scadder fuels the wish to buy plots of Eden by a seeming reluctance to sell, and Jonas uses exactly the same means to stimulate Pecksniff's appetite for investment. Awareness of lack functions always to intensify desire.

This mechanism of desire is the fundamental difference between the old-established firm of Chuzzlewit and the brand-new Anglo-Bengalee Company. Corporate capitalism flourishes not upon the individual self-interest of an entrepreneurial owner-capitalist, but by entrapping and stimulating the desires of thousands. The insurance business feeds upon desire for security and fear of death and distress; it exerts a powerful attraction, especially in times of acute economic struggle for survival. However, the functioning of all forms of speculative capitalism is more aggressively active than this, and is well represented in the characterization of Montague Tigg. Tigg is depicted as constructing himself into a social ideal – an Absolute Subject; he is a larger-than-life projection of opulent, worldly success. Every facet of his designer appearance, from his glossy hair to his glowing waistcoat and bejewelled fingers, is a signifier intended to impress but one signified – wealth. This Absolute Ego-Ideal functions, as always, to interpellate subjects. The ostentatious plenitude of Tigg reinforces a sense of lack in those who behold him at a distance, and this felt lack intensifies their desire. By allowing investors 'freely' to give him their money and thus buy (at a cost many can ill-afford) the privilege of being associated with such a glorious enterprise, Tigg acts like a glittering magic mirror promising to reflect his lustre back upon them. Thus the ordinary clients in the outer offices of the Anglo-Bengalee company are, at one and the same time, overawed and intimidated by the swift-passing spectacle of the Chairman being ceremoniously conducted to his opulent suite of rooms, and yet filled themselves with a vicarious sense of delightful importance (432).

In this speculative world, style and packaging have become art forms: Tigg boasts of his genius in 'the ornamental department' (429). Signification is wrenched free from any restraining connection to referents, running to a weed-like excess which constructs reified fantasy worlds floating upon emptiness, corresponding to nothing in the material universe. Such is the dream of Eden with its 'banks, churches, cathedrals, marketplaces' – simply a net of words to entangle vulnerable desire. In England the whole conspicuous self-advertizing presentation of the Anglo-Bengalee is without foundation – a designer-package for public consumption. In America the trend is to 'make commerce one huge lie and mighty theft'; back home Tigg insists 'don't say truth . . . It's so like humbug' (274, 441). Once set free from connection to material reality, the language of advertizing generates its own endlessly reproducing energies. Signs are caught up into a second-order system of signification in which concrete consumer signifieds are transposed into automatic signifiers of nonmaterial desire. Thus the vast red waistcoat displayed by the porter of the Anglo-Bengalee signifies 'Respectability, competence, property in Bengal or anywhere else . . . all expressed in that one garment' (431). In the language of consumer capitalism all desires are obtainable by wealth. Love, veneration, grief can all be signified by consumer goods: 'Oh!' cries Mr Mould, 'do not let us say that gold is dross, when it can buy such things as these' (323).

Thus mimetic representation (and diegetic commentary in the American sections) functions to articulate and explore some of the repressed anxieties aroused by hegemonic valorization of unrestrained individualism in the struggle for survival of the 1840s. In so doing, the text constructs a critique of the dangers of speculative capitalism still relevant in the late 1980s. Both eras are characterized by an aggressive assertion of self-interest and of wealth acquisition. In *Martin*

Chuzzlewit this is presented as encouraging a perilous unleashing of destructive energy — the force of desire is seized and impelled into the service of death. Moreover, the spread of speculative culture is related convincingly to an increased concern with presentation over substance, playing upon the vulnerabilities of common hopes and fears. The effect, articulated in the speech images of the text, is a dislocation of signification from material reality and the construction of the second order language of advertizing, in which money and consumer goods become signifiers of our non-material desires.

However, alongside this textual impulse to unmask the ideal of competitive individualism, is the moral plot centring upon Tom Pinch, and the imaginary 'solution' this offers functions to soften the radical edge of this criticism. As has been frequently noticed, Tom Pinch is constructed as an idealized opposition to the forms of excess in both fictional worlds of the novel. His friend, John Westlock, articulates the complete contrast between Tom and characters like Jonas or Tigg: 'You haven't half enough of the devil in you. Half enough! You haven't any' (21). In fact, the representation of Tom conforms very closely to the typical attributes of the womanly ideal. His discourse constructs an image of total self-repression; he is never happier than when sitting in a draught, or giving away carefully-saved money, or deprecating his own worth. Masochism seems the underlying impulse of the characterization, a complete opting out of the struggle for survival. Despite coy hints in the text concerning Tom's sexual desire for Mary, the repression of it seems more natural than any impulse towards fulfilment. Even the name 'Pinch' suggests a narrowing down or constraint of the life instincts. Tom expresses anger twice in the novel and on both occasions it is in response to expressions of contempt for his poverty and humble birth. On neither occasion does Tom lose control of himself, and significantly he claims: 'I speak without passion' (547). Thus Tom's function in the novel is identical to the ideological 'solution' of the womanly ideal; he offers a reassuring model of both sexual and social docility.

That the characterization is invested also with Dickens's desire for a fantasy ego-ideal is suggested by the identifying childhood reading and by Tom's pride in a grandmother who, like Dickens's, was a 'gentleman's housekeeper' (70, 22). The fulsome Carlylean apostrophes which shower praise upon Tom's unassuming head assuage unsatisfied desire in Dickens himself for moral approbation and social esteem. However, the straining rhetoric which characterizes the representation of Tom Pinch suggests that this identification with an ego-ideal of social and psychic constraint is a willed effort. The inflated prose, like the discourses of Tigg and Pecksniff, betrays a lack of referent – it corresponds to no reality beyond the verbal image.[13] While Dickens was producing the text of *Martin Chuzzlewit*, with its concern with unleashed energies, he wrote to a friend, 'I have a strong spice of the devil in me; and when I am assailed, as I think falsely or unjustly, my red hot anger carries me through it bravely'.[14] The insight arising from this perception of a positive energizing force of anger deconstructs the ideal of constraint projected through the figure of Tom Pinch. Masochistic suppression of desire is as destructive as unrestrained assertion; both lead to death. Tom Pinch, like others of Dickens's idealized characters, is in the grip of the death instincts, moving irresistibly away from the materiality of life, to be borne off finally in the sentimental rhetoric of the novel's concluding paragraph.

The character of Tom Pinch represents only the most obvious ideological 'solution' in the text. In effect, it merely offers to replace one hegemonic ideal (individualistic pursuit of wealth) with another closely implicated with it: the myth of moral progress, whereby the inner virtues of those like Tom Pinch are ultimately recognized and rewarded in material advancement, if not prosperity. However, the text also constructs a genuinely oppositional and radical ideological 'solution'. Moreover, this is an alternative perspective founded upon a positive sense of anger as a strategy of survival, and upon an assertion and celebration of the commonality of life rather than an opting out of struggle.

From the beginning, in Dickens's texts, the most challenging representations of anger are to be found in female characters. This is not to deny that many of these presentations subscribe shamelessly to the dominant hysterical woman myth by depicting characters, like Charity Pecksniff, as wilfully evoking their own passion. Additionally, anger in such single female characters is cruelly caricatured as part of their spinsterhood. They are bony, spiteful, and man-hungry; thus feminine anger and sexual desire are linked and jointly scourged by ridicule. However, in other cases, where the anger is connected with resistance to oppression, its subversive insights are validated by the passionate energy imparted into the speech image it constructs. The earliest example is of a quick-tempered woman's tirade at a drunken lout represented in the 'Pawnbrokers' episode in *Sketches*: 'What do you strike the boy for, you brute . . . do you think he's your wife, you willin? . . . Your poor dear wife as you uses worser nor a dog – strike a woman – you a man . . . I wish I had you – I'd murder you, I would, if I died for it!' (192). This is the first of a whole series of angry, fighting women in Dickens's texts, culminating in the splendidly subversive rage of Fanny Dorrit.

The speech images of all these later characters share the four dominant qualities already manifest in that quotation from *Sketches*: the anger is articulated from a working-class point of view, the discourse is represented as a powerful force of energy, the antagonism is directed at men as inherent oppressors, and there is a strong bond of fellow-feeling for other women. The class basis of women's anger as a means of survival is not difficult to comprehend. Working-class women were at the end of the line of social and political powerlessness – even their men could abuse them. Henry Mayhew acknowledged that while he met many young male urchins sustaining themselves on the streets, he did 'not hear of any girls who had run away from their homes having become street sellers only. They more generally fall into a course of prostitution' (I. 469). Moreover, among the street urchins he observed that 'the boy's opinion of the girl seems to be that she is made to help *him*, or to supply gratification to his passions', and, upon even the suspicion of an offence 'the "gals" are sure to be beaten cruelly and savagely by their "chaps" ' (I. 457–7). In this kind of world the playful resistance of a Sam Weller or an Artful Dodger is impossible. The only viable strategy of survival is an ever-ready anger; instead of parody and laughter, a burst of aggressive verbal energy. 'Poverty had made my mother sharp as well as careful', wrote a former housemaid in an account of her life.[15] It is this hard-pressed quality of 'sharpness' which Dickens emphasized in his representation of angry women. Nevertheless, anger is shown also as a strategy for maintaining self-respect. The simmering indignation represented in these characters expresses an insistence that they do matter, that they do have a claim to regard and dignity.

The sense of fellowship for other women can be seen also as growing out of real class experience. In their struggle to survive, women looked to other women for encouragement and help. The working-class tradition of co-operation may well have its roots in the sisterly care for their own kind embraced by the womenfolk. Dickens's texts express no ambivalence in the presentation of this quality.[16] In *Chuzzlewit*, Mrs Todgers is represented as 'looking sharp' after self-interest, and yet 'among the sordid strivings of her life' she maintained a 'secret door with "Woman" written on the spring' which offers Merry Chuzzlewit sympathy and shelter from the trials of her married life (583). Tied closely to the struggle for survival, women strove to create by their friendships a small oasis of sympathy, more trusting and gentle than the outside world. Such fellowship not only encouraged women to endure hardship, it also gave a sense of worth in a world where elsewhere they were ignored or repressed.

Sairey Gamp is one of Dickens's most splendid comic characters, and for this reason she often seems a timeless figure. However, the strength of the presentation resides in its basis in a precise class culture. Sairey's construction as comic heroine rests as securely upon knowledge of the struggle for survival in mean city streets as does the construction of the earlier comic hero, Sam Weller. The conditions of Sairey's fictional existence are as brutal as that of any of the other poor women Dickens represents in his fiction. She is depicted as having married a violent, drunken husband who knocked out her teeth, and whose drinking reduced them to penury. Sairey is only fortunate in having a trade by which to maintain herself, although not without the ever-present spectre of poverty should patients fail to materialize. The recurring references in her discourse to her slender means may be intended to soften up listeners, but equally they reflect the grip of economic necessity which, in the real world, pressed continually upon the Victorian working class. 'It is not an easy matter, gentlemen, to live when you are left a widder woman' she says (319).

If we tend to forget the economic conditions which shape Sairey Gamp's fictional struggle for existence, it is because the representation constructs a woman who fights back. Gamp knocks out her teeth, but when he dies Sairey revenges them by selling his remains to science! This pragmatic opportunism marks all her social dealings in the story. She gets her way peaceably if she can, but forcibly if she must. Almost her first entry into the novel evokes this dual quality; she comes 'sidling and bridling' upon Pecksniff and Jonas, declaring her readiness to 'feel for them as has their feelings tried' but adding a steely underlying hint that she has 'rules and regulations . . . which cannot be broke through' (319). The rhetorical devices of her speech image construct a continual edge of aggressiveness which dominates the characterization. The various configurations deployed in her discourse are consistently insistent, argumentative, and assertive. One of Sairey's most frequent linguistic mannerisms is the phrase 'if ever' or 'as ever', as in 'the last Monday evening fortnight as ever dawned', or 'for if ever a woman lived' (403). These formations impart a continual sense of insistence to Sairey's character discourse, as if implicitly expecting and countering contradiction. Other persistent patterns are more overtly argumentative. Sairey has a liking for rhetorical but aggressive questions, and for emphatic assertions and exclamations like 'ex-cuge me, if you please' (625) and 'I do assure you!'(464).

However, the most striking quality of Gampian discourse is its energy. Like nearly all of Dickens's angry women, Sairey's verbal power is represented as the means of maintaining her own space in a world of competitive struggle. In whatever social situation she is shown, Mrs Gamp seizes verbal dominance and in this way is never interpellated into the discourse of another and thus brought under their control. Sairey, with the help of Mrs Harris, insists on constituting herself. This capacity is represented most splendidly in response to a threat of hostility by Jonas Chuzzlewit. Male aggression is represented as completely drenched in a passionate outflow of words aimed at imposing a firm sense of Sairey's autonomy. The speech opens with a sarcastic assertion of dignity ('I hope, sir, . . . as no bones is broke by me and Mrs Harris a-walkin' down upon a public wharf'), moves on without pause for breath to her generally recognized worth ('I've been sought arter'), and independence ('I maintains my indepency . . . which I will till death'), and concludes with an uncompromising threat ('Don't try no impognician with the nuss, for she will not abear it!') (630–1).

Mrs Gamp also resembles other angry women characters in Dickens's fiction in that this aggression is directed towards men. The patients she is represented as ill-treating are all male, while the text implies that female patients generally return for each subsequent addition to their families. In the episode on the wharf, she is depicted as poking Tom Pinch with her umbrella, calling him 'Booby', but addressing Ruth as 'my dear young creetur'(624). Of the steam boat which attracts her animosity she declares, 'one might easy know you was a man's invention, from your disregardlessness of the weakness of our naturs' (626). Although her outward demeanour towards Jonas Chuzzlewit is presented as diplomatic, narrative discourse clearly suggests that she feels real sympathy for his wife. Despite the insensitive caricaturing of Charity Pecksniff and the American women in the novel, the presentation of Merry Chuzzlewit's victimization and that of Mary and Ruth has to be seen as a response to the debate over the treatment and role of women going on at the time. There is at least an implicit recognition in the text that the powerlessness of women – their enforced passivity – rendered them particularly vulnerable within a culture dominated by aggressive competition. Old Martin Chuzzlewit points out starkly the extent of women's powerlessness in relation to men: 'Remember that from your bridal hour to the day which sees you brought as low as these [graves], and laid in such a bed, there will be no appeal against him' (397). The recurring bird imagery which links Merry to the imprisoned sparrows in Poll Sweedlepipe's shop, destined as target practice to sporting gentlemen in the city, underlines women's vulnerability to male sexuality and aggression. Moreover, the mimetic force of the text subversively undercuts the submissive, feminine ideal represented in the characters of Mary and little Ruth, insisting that gentleness will provide no safeguard for women against such a fate. Only a Sairey Gamp can effectively stand up to a Jonas, and it is only her ever-ready anger which can protect women in a world where there is no appeal against male oppression.

In a novel articulated upon these oppositional impulses of anger and restraint, death and energy, the character of Sairey Gamp, midwife and watcher by the dead, implies a pivotal significance. Gampian discourse certainly gives death its due – 'it's what we must all come to' – she insists (315). However, in her 'highest walk of art' Sairey is a deliverer of life, and it is Eros that she is represented as consistently serving. Even at the undertaker's, Sairey's character discourse fixes upon marriage, and the amorous insinuations of the language are depicted as so inflaming Mr Mould's sexual passions that before long he is pinching his wife and taking her onto his knee.

Moreover, Mrs Gamp's language, like Sam Weller's, is characterized by a metonymic and celebratory expansiveness. Her narratives flow along lines of fluid contiguity, able to embrace all the contingent randomness of human life – 'a Punch's show . . . a chimbley sweep, a newfunlan dog, or a drunkin man, a-comin round the corner' (462) – all can be accommodated within the openness of Gampian discourse. Structured thus by contiguity, her speech constructs a persistent challenge to the closure of obsessive self-interest. In addition, the hegemonic discourses of reason and morality are mocked in the parodic anti-logic of such worthy conclusions as 'never . . . will I set by, and not stand up, don't think it' (403); 'sech is life. Vich likeways is the hend of all things' (462); and 'Rich folks may ride on camels, but is an't so easy for 'em to see out of a needle's eye. That is my comfort, and I hope I knows it' (407). Mrs Gamp's idiosyncratic pronunciation is regulated also by metonymic slippage – by close shifts in sounds, as in 'confusion' to 'confugion' (626). But in a world of proliferating signs without referents, Sairey's speech 'confugions' point warningly to the arbitrary nature of all signifiers.

Her mode of existence in the world, despite the ever-ready passion of anger, is represented equally as one of expansiveness. 'Gamp is my

name, and Gamp my natur' she says, and the generous vowel sound
contrasts strikingly with that of 'Pinch' (422). Sairey's room is
accessible to the street, her window being easily reached by walking
sticks, pebbles, and fragments of tobacco pipe. She and her belongings
have an irresistible tendency to spread themselves metonymically into
surrounding areas; she makes a cupboard of her patient's coat, storing
her nightbottle, 'an ingun or two and a little tea and sugar' in the
pockets (466). Above all, Sairey's embrace of life is expressed in her
appetite. Not even Tony Weller is represented as eating and drinking
with more gusto. Gampian discourse is punctuated with epicurean
catalogues of the delights of food: 'I could pick a little bit of pickled
salmon, with a nice little sprig of fennel and a sprinkling of white
pepper. I takes new bread, my dear, with jest a little pat of fresh butter,
and mossel of cheese' (411).

But does all this make Sairey Gamp part of the dangerously
unrestrained force of aggressive individualism in the novel, with her
anger allying her to Jonas's destructive violence, and her proliferating
speech to Tigg and Pecksniff in spawning a weed-like surface of false
signs as a trap for unwary desire? That this is intended is suggested by
her inclusion among those censured during the moral pantomime
ending enacted by old Martin. However, as with the presentation of
Tom Pinch, the interplay of character discourse functions to challenge
the narrative's ideological 'solution' as proffered in the moral plot.
Gampian discourse is actually very different from that of Tigg or
Pecksniff, and the dialogic contact between them is one of opposition.
Whereas their discourses are characterized by rhetorical abstraction (as
is much of the diegetic moral commentary), hers is marked by concrete
particularity. These other discourses in the text construct an
illusionary language of desire, pulling away from the world of reality
in pursuit of deceptive idealizations. Sairey's language, by contrast,
insists upon the materiality of everyday life. Mr Gill 'would back his
wife agen Moore's Almanac, to name the very day and hour, for
ninepence farden' (462). Mrs Harris resides 'through the square and up
the steps a-turnin' round by the tobacker shop' (624), and carries 'at
this present hour' Sairey's 'two single and two double' teeth 'along
with two cramp-bones, a bit o' ginger, and a grater like a blessed
infant's shoe, in a tin, with a little heel to put the nutmeg in' (705).

Of course, the whole Harris saga *is* as fictional as Eden. It is a device
to produce false testimony of Mrs Gamp's excellence. However, in
contrast to the Eden fraud, the text makes no suggestion that anyone is
taken in but Sairey herself. This is because it is Sairey's desire which the

images meet. In a competitive, struggling world in which only anger and aggression can protect women and the working class from exploitation and oppression, Sairey's speech image constructs an imaginative ego-ideal based upon very different values. The Harris fiction becomes a comic celebration of ordinary human life based upon the oppositional, non-hegemonic ethics of mutual affection and co-operation. The proliferating young Harrises cock an optimistic snub at dismal Malthusian projections of excessive population. Unlike Jonas, Mr Harris is 'the best of husbands' wearing his wife's likeness 'faithful next his heart till the colour run' (701) and is so distressed at the birth of their First that he 'stopped his ears in a empty dog-kennel' while she is told 'to ease her mind, his 'owls was organs' (748). Sairey's character discourse constructs herself as privileged participant in this loving community, having 'know'd Mrs Harris five-and-thirty year ... [and] stood her friend in all her troubles, great and small' (752–3). Sairey's final image of the Harrises is of 'that dear woman ... expectin of me at this minnit ... a-lookin' out of winder down the street, with little Tommy Harris in her arms, as calls me his own Gammy' (755). This transforming imaginary spectacle of self as part of a loving, mutually-helping society, sustains a sense of self-respect, amidst the sordid, grasping reality imposed by the world of necessity.

The presentation of Mrs Gamp, therefore, reverses the familiar fictional figure of the mad woman in the attic. Mrs Gamp's anger is maintained in the world as a strategy of self-survival and self-interpellation. It is in her imaginative construction of self that she creates an unaggressive identity. As with the urchin characters, this process of self-construction is offered as convivial spectacle. Sairey's characterization partakes of the duality of the carnivalesque mask; to the world of competitive struggle she unveils its own image of death, but facing the other way she proffers us the comic inclusive laughter of life. In contrast to the ego-ideal constructed in the presentation of Tom Pinch, with its impulse towards death as escape from struggle, the ideal of conviviality created in the character of Sairey is based upon material practice. It derives from the utopian values of sisterhood, co-operation, and community practiced by working-class women in their support for each other in their struggles. Sairey gains a sense of self-worth from the regard reflected on her by the gaze of a known and loving community which she has created. There is a telling difference between this convivial construction of self and the representation of both Tigg's and Pecksniff's conscious remaking of their public images, narcissistically, in front of a mirror (492, 652).

Read in this way, the figure of Sairey Gamp is timely rather than timeless, suggesting that women – that all oppressed and marginalized groups – need to retain contact with their anger as a strategy for sustaining self-respect and as means of resisting guilt-inflicting and depoliticizing interpellation. The ideological solution the moral plot imposes on the problems of individualistic excess explored in the novel deconstructs itself. The womanly ideal of Tom Pinch warns of the danger of totally suppressing desire. But Sairey's transforming fiction within the fiction suggests that the force of desire does not need to be channelled into the aggressive individualism fostered by a capitalist culture, nor into the self-deluding fantasies upon which capitalist speculation feeds. Desire can be displaced more positively into the unifying impulse of the life instincts to create a utopian vision of community, where narcissistic regard broadens into co-operative endeavour and mutually reflecting esteem. That this vision can be projected only in the chinese box form of a double fiction suggests the dangerously subversive nature of these values within the dominant individualistic culture of early Victorian England.

Notes

1. Quoted in J. F. C. Harrison, *Early Victorian Britain 1831–51* (1979) pp. 30–1.
2. For the details in this paragraph I have drawn upon the accounts in Harold Perkins, *The Origins of Modern English Society 1780–1880* (1972) pp. 107–124, and R. K. Webb, *Modern England* (1969) pp. 261–7.
3. Dickens has been seen as anachronistic in depicting so few manufacturers in his novels as opposed to financiers like Ralph Nickleby, Mr Dombey, etc. However, recent research suggests that Dickens was, in fact, providing an accurate representation. In *The Rise of Respectable Society* (1988), F. M. L. Thomson outlines the 'new orthodoxy' of history that until the 1860s, at least, large fortunes were made, not in manufacturing, but in the traditional activities of banking, commerce, law, brewing, and overseas trade (p. 161).
4. Webb, p. 267. In a parallel way, in the 1980s, wider share ownership is perceived ideologically as a means of propagating an enterprise culture.
5. The article in the *Christian Observer* also contained a description of the ferocious American bowie knife mentioned in *Chuzzlewit*. Moreover, Miss Sedgewick's claims for American prosperity provoked one reader into protesting in the next issue, 'America is not an Eden' (1843, p. 28).
6. Sigmund Freud, *Civilization and Its Discontents*, in the Pelican Freud Library Vol. 12 (1985), p. 314. Freud's fullest account of the death and life

instincts is in *Beyond the Pleasure Principle* in the Pelican Freud Library, Vol. 11.

7. *Civilization and Its Discontents*, p. 313.

8. *Civilization and Its Discontents*, p. 313.

9. This perceived connection between women's discontent and general political unrest was stated explicitly by a *Westminster* reviewer: 'Many are disposed to put down with a strong hand, every suggestion of possible improvement in the condition of women, regarding it as part and parcel of the great rebellious movement against all constituted authority, which is said to be the peculiar wickedness of the age in which we live' (53 (1850), p. 516). In *Shirley* (1848) Charlotte Bronte also makes a deliberate link between sexual and social discontent: 'I observe that to such grievances as society cannot readily cure, it usually forbids utterance... Old maids, like the houseless and unemployed poor, should not ask for a place and an occupation in the world' (Chapter 22).

10. A theoretical analysis of the way literary texts function to displace ideological tensions in the real world onto imaginary contradictions soluble within the substitutions of the text is offered by Etienne Balibar and Pierre Macherey, 'On Literature as an Ideological Form' reprinted in *Untying the Text*, pp. 79–99.

11. A parallel passage occurs when Pecksniff forces his lecherous intent upon Mary after which he is represented as 'trying to hide himself within himself' (483). Indeed, the characterization of Pecksniff is largely concerned with unrestrained sexuality, although he is accused also of having 'traded' in young Martin 'as a speculation' (801).

12. The *Edinburgh Review* later corroborated the accuracy of Dickens's prophetic representation of speculation in Assurance Companies: 'nothing could more forcibly illustrate the credulity of the public' than the ephemeral nature of these societies, it wrote (109 (1859), 47).

13. Alexander Welsh, in *From Copyright to Copperfield* (1987) draws attention to this identity between Pecksniffian discourse and narrative discourse, especially in exclaiming the merits of Tom Pinch, p. 27.

14. *Letters*, III (1974), 493.

15. Quoted in *Useful Toil: Autobiographies of Working People*, edited by John Burnett (1977), p. 215.

16. The most explicit approval comes in *Bleak House*, in Esther's tribute to the brickmakers' wives: 'I thought it very touching to see these two women, coarse and shabby and beaten, so united; to see what they could be to one another; to see how they felt for one another, how the heart of each to each was softened by the hard trials of their lives' (109).

Part II:
Mechanisms of Submission

3

David Copperfield: Alienated Writer

Even without Dickens's autobiographical confession to Forster, *David Copperfield* would stand apart from the rest of his fiction. Most obviously, it seems to mark a turning away from the sprawling public world represented in his previous texts, and again in subsequent novels, towards a closer focus upon the private, individual experience of a psychological narrative. The representation of a personalized narrative voice contributes to the characteristic tone of *David Copperfield*; its sense of dreamlike intensity unattached to Dickens's usual mimetic representation of a busy material world. Many narrative episodes, especially in the early chapters, convey the hyper-reality and emotional charge of dream experience, and indeed, 'dream' is a word massively reiterated in the text. Perhaps it is not surprising, therefore, that displacement is a feature of the writing, with characters' identities exhibiting the kind of shifting substitutions we find in dreams. The unease articulated in the earlier text of *Martin Chuzzlewit* over excessive individualistic energy as a destructive force becomes, in *Copperfield*, a fear or recoil from almost all forms of active struggle.

For this reason, the apparent retreat into the private should be read as a continuation of the ideological issues materialized in *Martin Chuzzlewit*. More even than that earlier novel, *David Copperfield* offers itself as a politically innocent text, whilst it deploys a system of fictional representation which, by means of substitutions and displacements, constructs an imaginary 'solution' for pressing ideological tensions in the real world of the late 1840s. The use of the first person narrative form encourages a particularly strong reader identification in the offered resolution. This ability to contain and appease social anxiety may explain some of the immediate and lasting popularity of the novel.

Martin Chuzzlewit was written in the aftermath of the second Chartist petition, amidst a sense of social fermentation, population excess, and an explosion of aggressive competitive energy in capitalist expansion and speculative ventures. *Copperfield* was written during a period which seemed, and seems still, to mark the culmination of those unleashed forces. In February 1848, a revolution in Paris toppled the monarchy of Louis Philippe and established a republic proclaiming socialist principles. Subsequently, revolutions broke out all over Europe. In Britain, the Chartists were encouraged by these events, and by the continued severe social distress exacerbated by the Irish Famine, to present their third petition amid fears of massive public demonstrations to be backed by threats of physical force. In the event, the huge army of petitioners expected to converge on the capital dwindled to a peaceful, good-humoured crowd of around 25,000, massively outnumbered by the 200,000 special constables sworn in to protect property and the constitution. This was the last, already enfeebled, uprising of the great vigorous tide of social protest engendered earlier in the decade. However, this ebbing away of energy only became clear with hindsight; at the time fear of a working-class revolution was very real among the middle and upper classes. The *Westminster Review* attested to the widespread belief that the 'artisan population' was biased towards 'extreme political opinion'(48 (1847), 426). The *Methodist Magazine* wrote with 'grief and indigna-tion at the wicked attempts . . . to create revolutionary agitation and disturbance' (1848, p. 1002*).

A modern historian has written of Chartism that it 'marked the end of an old world, not the beginning of a new'.[1] Significantly the end of the 1840s saw also the climax and first ebb of competitive capitalist energies. With the end of the decade the accelerating economic growth passed its peak and, although disguised by the expanding colonial markets for British goods, increasingly from the 1850s entrepreneurial and technical innovation bypassed Britain to be developed by foreign competitors like Germany and America.[2]

This economic shift needs to be related to the hegemonic interaction ensuing at the time between two competing ideologies, leading to the accommodation and containment of the individualistic competitive ideal within an upper-class system of values. Middle-class insistence that wealth was a reliable signifier of virtue, while poverty was the outward sign of moral lack, constituted a most effective social myth for constructing its own class identity through difference, and for justifying the condition and status of the working class as the result of their own irresponsible degradation. However, the ideological need constantly to emphasize the respectability of outward manner inevitably fostered vulnerability to the seductive attractions of gentility. This vulnerability was the means by which the upper class recaptured hegemonic initiative while apparently relinquishing political control. The nature and outcome of this hegemonic conflict is figured more accurately as a marriage than as a war, with both parties seeking to gain from the alliance.[3] The repeal of the Corn Laws in 1846 resolved the only important clash of interests between the two classes, and in any case, by the end of the 1840s, many landowners were heavily involved as capitalists in mining, railways, and other industries. Moreover, the spectre of working-class revolution pressed home the advantages of closing ranks upon the nightmare of a looting and violent mob so recently seen in control of the streets of Paris. The ego-ideal of gentility offered a self-image even more securely differentiated from the uncouth labouring classes than that of the questing entrepreneurial Absolute Subject. Thus, 'at the moment of its triumph, the entrepreneurial class turned its energies to reshaping itself in the image of the class it was supplanting'.[4]

This ideological accommodation was not only the result of a recoil from revolutionary energies stirred up in the working class by events on the continent and the distress of the 'hungry decade'. There seems also to have been a recoil of the competitive capitalist drive itself, perhaps, in part, a reaction to the unsavoury spectacle of over-speculation, unbridled greed, and worship of wealth which the decade of capitalist triumph had exhibited. For the first time the *Christian Observer* sounded a note of criticism against the 'present busy, anxious, aspiring, money-getting state of society' (1847, p. 584). Even the *Edinburgh Review*, the staunchest supporter by the late 1840s of political economy, felt moved to criticize the 'recent insanity of speculation' in the commercial classes and the 'disastrous con-sequences' of a 'haste to be rich' attitude among capitalists (88 (1948), 397). In 1848, John Stuart Mill published his *Principles of Political Economy*, and although he argued the need for competition still as a means to greater prosperity for all, the tone was very different from the unambiguous enthusiasm of his father's generation of Utilitarians in early issues of the *Westminster*. His warning against the result of unchecked capitalism conveyed an unflattering picture of the entre-preneurial ideal, while his language bears a striking resemblance to the emotive imagery of *Chuzzlewit*.

I confess I am not charmed with the ideal of life held out by those who think that the normal state of human beings is that of struggling to get on; that the trampling, crushing, elbowing, and treading on each other's heels, which form the existing type of social life, are the most desirable lot of human kind, or anything but the disagreeable symptoms of one of the phases of industrial progress.[5]

According to a recent account of British industrial decline the ideal of 'progress' so ideologically powerful in earlier years received a check as the century progressed and 'was more and more pushed back by the contrary ideals of stability, tranquility, closeness to the past, and nonmaterialism'[6] – ideals which permeate *David Copperfield*. The most powerful ideological apparatus for constructing subjects in conformity to this new ego-ideal or Absolute Subject was the public school system which was established and consolidated by the last years of the 1840s. Looking back in 1861, the Clarendon Commission on Public Schools recognized as their finest achievement that 'they have had perhaps the largest share in moulding the character of an English Gentleman' (*Edinburgh Review*, 120 (1864), 180).

Most of these cultural, ideological and economic shifts were barely perceptible tendencies in 1848–9. However, the text of *David Copperfield* picks up all these gathering concerns, displacing them into a seemingly apolitical psychological narrative, which, like its hero, appears to shrink from political pronouncement. The fact that the text works so hard at neutralizing and disguising its ideological conflicts suggests that these may touch upon areas of fear and anxiety within Dickens himself. As in *Martin Chuzzlewit*, the point of intersection between the social world and the individual subject is again to be found in the focus of opposition between the life and the death instincts.

The very first sentence of *David Copperfield* is marked by ambiguity and splitting: 'Whether I shall turn out to be the hero of my own life, or whether that station will be held by anybody else, these pages must show' (1). While the emphatic imperative mood of that final clause, 'these pages must show', seems to assert a willed intention of self-creation as hero, the product of narrative construction, the earlier verb phrase, 'Whether I shall turn out', implicitly admits a more passive role in any making of the self, since it falls back upon the metaphor of a mould shaping the subject by external pressure. Moreover, the doubt about status engendered by the initial interrogative word undercuts the confidence of the final intentional clause, seeming to promise narrative not as heroic self-construction, but as confession of lack. Thus the narrating 'I', no less than the narrated 'I', is a divided self, intent simultaneously upon self-making and upon unmaking and unmasking. This self-alienation and self-confusion involves David Copperfield's narrative discourse with a persistent threat of dis-integration, pulling against the cohesive influence of its unitary tone and plot structure.

Nevertheless, the first narrated representation of self is one of primary unity; of the child at the centre of its universe whose circumference is its mother. David as subject of the narrative is first aware of self moving unsteadily between the two mother figures of his childhood (11). The two Claras represent the first displacement among many in the text of the desired maternal image, split in this initial instance between the sexually desirable Oedipal mother and the pre-Oedipal nurturing and protective mother in the form of Peggotty.[7] This representation of earliest experience is characterized by the static spacial and temporal unity of dream or of the unconscious; there is no sense of linear progress between either different moments or different places. The present tense and repetition of deictic phrases such as 'And now I see' or 'Here is' deny causal narrative movement, conveying the tableau-like clarity of dream sequence. Social unity is also a feature of this phase, for 'Peggotty is quite our companion, when her work is done and we are alone' (12). The narrator later names this experience of primary unity a 'dream', recognizing by that term both its haunting power in the imagination and its subsequent unrealizable elusiveness: 'every object I looked at, reminded me of the happy old home, which was like a dream I could never dream again! The days when my mother and I and Peggotty were all in all to one another' (93). Still later in the narrative the sense of unappeasable lack engendered by this primary loss is admitted more fully. 'The old unhappy feeling pervaded my life. It was deepened, if it were changed at all; but it was as undefined as ever . . . there was always something wanting. . . . What I missed, I still regarded – I always regarded – as something that had been a dream of my youthful fancy; that was incapable of realization' (594–5).

When disintegration threatens the unified childhood world, Peggotty, like the protective mother-figure she represents, carries David off to a substitute 'happy home'. Again the sequences in the text are narrated with a timeless dream quality. The child's pre-Oedipal phase of unity and plenitude is named by Lacan the Imaginary, to indicate that it exists before the imposition of the Reality Principle, and before experience is divided and named through difference within the Symbolic Order. At Yarmouth, there is a fantasy displacement of the absent, sexually desirable, mother onto Little Em'ly with her blue eyes and fluttering girlish figure. However, there is a difference; this home has been constructed in conscious opposition to the disintegrative forces of separation and death by the actively unifying compassion of Daniel Peggotty. At Yarmouth, David experiences unity as sociability and community:

> Little Em'ly had overcome her shyness, and was sitting by my side ... Mrs Peggotty, with the white apron, was knitting on the opposite side of the fire. Peggotty at her needlework was as much at home with St Paul's and the bit of wax candle as if they had never known any other roof. Ham, who had been giving me my first lesson in all-fours, was trying to recollect a scheme for telling fortunes with the dirty cards ... Mr Peggotty was smoking his pipe. I felt it was time for conversation and confidence (27–8).

The adult narrator, who as character is a successful author, interrupts his story so as to emphasize from the outset the lasting 'inheritance' of this phase of childhood as an influence throughout life, implicitly linking it to the imaginative and creative capacity of the writer, especially in terms of qualities named as pleasure, 'freshness' and 'gentleness' (11). These claims appear to receive support outwith narrative discourse from a sub-narrative which shadows David Copperfield's narrative, interacting with it dialogically to supplement, support and challenge the main narrative's assertions. Woven into the text of *David Copperfield* are fragmentary references to Matthew 18 which begins, like *Copperfield*, with a question about status. The disciples ask who will be greatest in the kingdom of heaven and for answer a little child is placed among them: 'Except ye be converted, and become as little children, ye shall not enter the kingdom of heaven'. The remainder of Matthew 18 parallels the main incidents of the novel, warning that for any who betray 'these little ones' it were better for him 'that he were drowned in the depths of the sea' and continues with the story of the good shepherd who goes off in search of the lost lamb, as Daniel Peggotty goes off to recover his lost 'little one', Em'ly.

The child's sense of being at the centre of a securely loving world is precarious. The primary unity of the Imaginary phase, before the imposition of the Reality Principle in the form of the Father's Law, is only maintained by projecting threats of disintegration to the margin. Typically, David's idyllic dreamlike early experience is fringed by fears of the dark, of death and violence – a repressed which returns in nightmares: 'I dream at night: as a man environed by wild beasts might dream of lions' (12). Similarly, along the margin of the flat where he dawdles in the sun with Em'ly, the sea prowls 'hungry' and 'cruel'. The wisps of straw floating down from the deserted rooks' nests insist upon the inevitability of loss and disintegration. With the return from Yarmouth the narrator recounts his moment of loss. In the Oedipal conflict with Murdstone, David is expelled from the centre of his world to its margin. From the infant dream of heroic omnipotence, he is recast as powerless and victimized. This separation from primary self had already been foreshadowed in the narrative when Murdstone tricked David into misnaming and confounding himself by proposing a toast 'Confusion to Brooks of Sheffield' (20). This is only the first of a series of renamings each of which compounds the separation and confusion of self. Significantly, 'Brooks' is a trade name; the Oedipal conflict marks the insertion of the child within the Law of the Father, within the public world of inequalities, power relations, and oppression. From this moment all private narratives become social.

To be childlike or powerless – 'one of these little ones' – in the world beyond the Imaginary dream of unity is to be humiliated, beaten, and broken. Creakle, the schoolmaster, a substitute father, is identified with Murdstone in the desire to experience power sensuously, even erotically, by the infliction of pain. The narrating subject of *David Copperfield* testifies bleakly to the absence of anger or parody as strategies of self-survival where terror breeds only servile imitation and collaboration: 'Mr Creakle cuts a joke before he beats him, and we laugh at it, – miserable little dogs, we laugh, with our visages as white as ashes, and our hearts sinking into our boots' (78). However, even before this, David, the narrated subject, has been broken by a yet more efficient system of psychological subjection. It was known as the Silent System and its aim was to 'turn out' individuals as guilty subjects. Its effect was described graphically by the *Edinburgh Review* in 1848:

> In that dread isolation – in that all but sepulchral silence, where, even in the brief intervals in which he leaves his cell to repair to an unsocial devotion, he is muffled in a hood that he may neither know others, nor be known; and, shod with felt, moves along the corridors with unechoing footsteps, as if already a disembodied spirit – it is hardly possible for him to decline what he has so long forgotten, the task of introspection and reflection; if not silenced for ever, the voice of conscience will be heard (86 (1847), 260).

Barring the added horror of the hood, this is a pretty good description of David's ordeal of isolation following his biting of

Murdstone. The five days of silence – 'the strange sensation of never hearing myself speak . . . seemed to quench me in gloom, and fear, and remorse' (51).

The subject reconstructed from this 'quenching' of self is confessional and conciliatory. The impulse of those outcast and marginalized is to subject themselves to conformity with the image of an Absolute Subject at the centre of power and authority. In Freudian terms, the child accommodates his submission to the castrating father by seeking identification with him. The social dimension of this process of self-remaking is articulated at its extreme in the character discourse of Uriah Heep, who conforms to the submissive image demanded of the working class, while identifying with the will to oppression. 'I am very 'umble to the present moment, Master Copperfield,' he tells David, 'but I've got a little power!' (491). The response of the evangelical journals to popular social unrest during 1847–8 was to intensify their emphasis upon duty, discipline, and obedience. The many long sermons printed on these themes reiterated and fused the obligation for total submission to Authority as God, State, and parent: an 'unreserved and uniform, constant and universal obedience' is required 'in individual, domestic, social, civic life'.[8] The speech images constructed by the character discourses of Murdstone and Creakle echo this repressive language. Murdstone labels tyranny 'firmness' and Creakle disguises it as 'duty' (42, 71).

However, as the text unfolds, the discourse of the narrating 'I', the adult Copperfield, begins to assume a shocking resemblance to that of Murdstone and of dominant repressive morality. Second only to the word 'dream', the word 'duty' increasingly encroaches upon the narrator's language. This moral discourse enacts a split between the narrated 'I' and the adult narrator whereby the latter imitates the role of Murdstone in condemning and punishing his younger self for 'a wayward boyhood', 'headlong passion', and lack of discipline (699, 822). By thus constructing a confessional narrative, the adult narrator is able simultaneously to fulfil the obligation for constant submission to authority and yet to experience identification with that power through his severe castigation of former self. Towards the end of the novel, the narrator's language of self becomes, at times, almost indistinguishable from the repentant, self-confessing autobiographies in the religious journals. As the narrated 'I' apparently becomes a successful writer, the narrator's discourse is characterized increasingly by the exclamatory, breastbeating style of evangelicalism with its use of clichèd biblical allusion: 'Oh, how had I strayed so far away!'; 'What I reaped I had sown' (716, 711). This construction of a confessional narrative retrospect pulls the plot structure into a unitary moral significance, shaped by the familiar causal pattern. The youthful recklessness of an 'undisciplined heart' is shocked and chastened by death of a loved one. The 'awakening' into sin and guilt results in repentance, a return to righteousness and eventual worldly reward.

There is a vast difference between the celebratory, gregarious, and playful self-making represented in the characterizations of Sam Weller and Sairey Gamp and this restrictive construction of self upon guilt and submission. The hegemonic myth of self-improvement enacts the subjection of subjects, offering only the closure of moral logic in place of the openness of creative self-making. David Copperfield's process of self-improvement after this spiritual crisis and rebirth is, typically, a detailed introspection and acknowledgement of 'sin'. 'I tried to get a better understanding of myself and be a better man ... [as] a means of making me more self-denying, more resolved, more conscious of myself, and my defects and errors' (700–1). But confession is a duplicitous narrative form. As with the confessions of 'defects and errors' in evangelical journals, the function of the moral plot structure of *David Copperfield* is to construct the narrator as triumphant hero of moral progress in his own life. The narrative testifies 'freely' to the growth, self-recognition, and self-regeneration of an autonomous subjectivity, while the first person form functions to draw the reader deeply and sympathetically into an identification with that private epic of inner conquest leading to worldly success.

However, the confessional quality of the text of *David Copperfield* is more multiply duplicitous than this. The child David is terrorized while so young that no resort to parody is possible; laughter merely imitates and propitiates the tyrant. Nevertheless, parody is present in the text in the form of confession – the confessions of Heep and Littimer (self-made men) subjected to a travesty of the Silent System. The discourse of the narrating 'I' is at its most moralistic and punitive in referring to these men, but by their parodic construction of themselves as moral heroes, they insert into the narrative a subversive confession of the duplicity or dishonesty of its own confessional form.

The novel has been criticized for making art 'so much a matter of moral duty'.[9] This is an astute insight; the imposition of unitary meaning upon the hero-subject the narrative constructs can only be maintained by constant repression of all that is other to that moral myth of self-making. What is most strongly repressed in the narrator's moral discourse is awareness of the inheritance from the Imaginary phase of childhood – that memory trace of gentleness and pleasure. Psychoanalytic theory suggests that desire to recreate this lost dream of infant plenitude is a major impulse behind artistic endeavour and attempts at visionary transformation of present realities.[10] The text of *Copperfield* traces an associative displacement of identity from the youthful sexually desirable mother, depicted metonymically in connection with flowers and gardens, to a feminine aspect of David's self called into consciousness by Steerforth and named by him 'Daisy', to David's first child-wife, 'Blossom'. Dora's death, therefore, represents by substitution the death of the youthful visionary self with those qualities of gentleness, freshness, and pleasure associated with the Imaginary phase of maternal plenitude and hence with the creative imagination. As already indicated, the moral hero reborn from this crisis of death mirrors the forbidding father far more than the sexual and creative mother.

Murdstone and Creakle are associated with trade, and this is the future mapped out for David as fictional subject. Murdstone's parting injunction holds out the possibility of self-making as individualist enterprise: 'To the young this is a world for action ... What is before you is a fight with the world' (130–1). However, although narrative discourse constructs David as hero of moral progress, there is a subtle slippage within it away from the concomitant ideal of material conquest of the world onto an heroic image actually opposed to notions of 'progress'. The first response of the narrative to the divisive imposition of Murdstone is the displacement of David into a community whose values oppose all that Murdstone signifies – Daniel Peggotty's visionary transformation of loss and separation into affectionate communality. The second response of David as character is identification with fictional heroes who 'never lost dignity' and 'kept alive my fancy and my hope' (48), and this represents a very different class affiliation. Once expelled from the Imaginary and impelled by the Law of the Father to an accommodation with the world of necessity, desire for imaginative transformation can only be encoded within the Symbolic Order – within those ideological images and ego-ideals offered by the social formation.

This encoding of desire within the Symbolic is illustrated in Little Em'ly's part visionary, part social image of her uncle as a 'gentleman' in a 'sky-blue coat with diamond buttons' (30). The 'solution' for both David's and Em'ly's sense of powerlessness and their visionary desire to transform present reality lies in identification with the social encodement of 'gentleman'. Steerforth, 'a person of great power' as

well as cultured charm, thus represents an irresistible Absolute Subject
– the hero as gentleman. David, as narrated character, is quick to
perceive that even Creakle is submissive before the social prestige of
the gentlemanly ideal. However, far from offering any transforming
social re-creation of the unity and plenitude of primary experience,
Steerforth is wholly implicated in the dominant order of the Symbolic.
His power is based upon the ability of the gentlemanly image to
signify difference and division. This function is crystallized as David
records the confrontation with impoverished Mr Mell: 'I could not
help thinking . . . what a noble fellow he was in appearance and how
homely and plain Mr Mell looked opposed to him' (84). It is the
character discourse of Steerforth which articulates most explicitly in
the text the repressive equation of external appearance with inner
sensibility; the marking of difference as justification for class
oppression. Shabby Mr Mell is not to be expected to feel inner
wounding as a result of public humiliation (86). Later, Steerforth
asserts that the rough skins of working-class people reliably indicated
their coarse, insensitive natures (251), and this class contempt is made
manifest in the betrayal and destruction of the community at
Yarmouth.

Narrative discourse clearly distances itself from the uncritical
adulation of the younger self for Steerforth. However, there is no such
ironic distancing from one marked feature of the narrator's language.
Along with moralistic assertion, David Copperfield's narrative
discourse is characterized by an obsessive marking of social division.
After escape from the perceived degradation of manual work, the
narrator's commentary persistently draws reader attention to class
differences as if under a compulsion thus to prevent slippage of social
identity. This fear of loss of status is articulated most overtly in the
representation of the youthful David's relations with waiters and
servants, who, absolutely without exception, function in the narrative
to threaten his sense of secure identity, so that he feels 'nobody stood
in any awe of me at all' (243). Only association with Steerforth, the
genuine gentleman, can check this disintegration of genteel self.
Within this discourse of class distinction, Peggotty is redesignated 'my
old nurse', and thereafter, whenever any of the Peggottys are referred
to, narrative discourse is meticulous in emphasizing signifiers of
deferential difference at each encounter. Pulling against rhetorical
needs for sustaining pathos and emotional intensity, the narrator
constantly draws reader attention to necessary distinctions of rank:
whatever the degree of tragedy, Mr Peggotty is represented as

removing his cap, carrying David's bags, and addressing him as 'Sir'. The only function of this aspect of narrative discourse is to construct the hero as gentleman through differentiation.

The process begins appropriately with a ritual rebirth and renaming; the plebian 'Davey' is re-interpellated by the clipped upper-class tone of 'Trotwood'. As in the real world of the late 1840s, the fictional *deus et machina* for performing the magic of social transformation is the public school with its emphasis on the classics and nonmaterial patrician values. Equally mirroring the trend in the real world is the progress from school into a professional career, in preference to one in industry or commerce. The choice of Doctors' Commons is made when Steerforth asserts that 'they plume themselves on their gentility there' (293). However, as with the construction of moral hero, so this narrative-making of the hero as English gentleman necessitates the repression of all that is other to this genteel identity. This involves the whole of the childhood experience of the world of work. When first admitted to the genteel enclosure of Dr Strong's school, David, as character, is so 'ashamed' of his knowledge of 'London life and London streets' that he is distrustful of his 'slightest look and gesture' as treacherous signifiers of his shameful secret (196). However, soon this past self is so repressed and split off from the remade self – captain and hero of the school – that 'that little fellow seems to be no part of me; I remember him as something left behind upon the road of life' (229).

Nevertheless, figures from this world of work and city streets continually haunt the margins of the narrative like a persistent return of the repressed. At every stage in his life David as character is liable to be assailed by some frenetic and menacing figure from the lower class. With the exception of the Peggottys, servants, waiters, tramps, and vagrants are represented as rapacious, aggressive, derisive, and discontented, from the boy with the donkey who races off with David's entire worldly goods, to the sturdy beggars prowling at the margin of Dr Strong's secluded garden. In the real world of 1848, fear-engendered class hostility depoliticized working-class unrest by constructing them as criminalized, and so degraded as to 'honour, truth, justice, and gratitude' as to be beneath even 'those stunted outcasts of the human race in New Zealand'. This 'plague of poverty and crime' wrote a commentator in the *Westminster Review* has 'penetrated into the body of the people' (48 (1847), 428). *The Times*, taking up the same subject, declared: 'The great thoroughfares "are alive" with beggars' (27 January 1848).This sense of a restless force of criminal life is reproduced throughout the text of *David Copperfield*, and most memorably in the depiction of David's nightmare journey to Dover where violent figures of the working class stretch out rapacious hands to claw him back and fasten him in his penury and powerlessness. So, in 1848, 'might a man environed by wild beasts dream of lions'.

The retreat from energy in the interpellation of hero as gentleman is expressed at a deep level of narrative structure. As well as class differentiation and moral assertion, the narrative discourse which constructs David Copperfield as hero is characterized by a figurative pattern of language. This centres upon the reiterated word 'dream', associations of death, and a chain of substitutions operating on the image of the desired mother. This dimension of narrative discourse could be termed an unconscious narrative which yet 'confesses' its psychic drama. According to Freud 'the aim of all life is death'; the strongest and most primitive drive is that of the death instincts impelling the organism back to the 'quiescence' of inanimate things.[11] In opposition to these 'destructive' instincts are the sexual instincts, the 'true life instincts' characterized by an impulse for union and community.[12] David Copperfield's desire for gentility is implicated in narrative discourse with an impulse towards death. The moment of the hero's birth, the journey from 'the land of dreams and shadows', is linked syntactically with death in the image of the father's grave, the 'ashes and dust' of which are the 'earthly bourne of all such travellers' (11).

For no reason at all in terms of plot or characterization, narrative discourse, strangely, constructs the existence of a ghostly unborn sister – a feminine version of self – who remains in this land of 'dreams'. This feminine self is summoned up in the homosexual relationship with Steerforth; in Steerforth's desire for David's imaginary sister, 'a pretty, timid, little, bright-eyed sort of girl' (76) – a transposition of narrative desire, moving by means of a series of substitutions through sister/ mother/Emily/Dora. This regressive impulse to return to unified identity with the desired mother of infancy by means of substitutions and retreat into dream, forms a recurring narrative pattern, suggesting the 'compulsion to repetition' by which Freud first recognized the working of the death instincts. Returning home from school to discover his mother with a new baby, David places his head 'down upon her bosom near the little creature that was nestling there' and wishes 'I had died then' (94). This desired identification and consummation is achieved by substitution in the death of both mother and baby: 'The mother who lay in the grave was the mother of my infancy; the little creature in her arms, was myself, as I had once been, hushed forever on her bosom' (115). Rebirth into the genteel self as 'Trotwood' re-enacts this regression to infancy (swaddled up in shawls like a baby) and death. Dr Strong's school, situated in a 'grave' building, is associated not with youthful vitality or any spirit of play, but with 'silence and retirement' (195). The narrated memory of schooldays is not of activity but of Sunday morning in the Cathedral with 'the earthy smell, the sunless air, the sensation of the world being shut out' (226). Entry into an adult career again exhibits this compulsion to retreat. In the vicinity of Doctors' Commons 'the noise of the city seemed to melt, as if by magic, into a softened distance', and David is very well 'satisfied with the dreamy nature of this retreat' (298, 301).

The underlying narrative impulse towards death finds its consummation in the union with Agnes. The representation of Dora rematerializes the youthful sexually desired mother, but Agnes represents the static perfection of the dead mother. That Agnes is constructed within the narrator's discourse in the figurative language of angels, cathedral stained glass, 'grave' light, tranquillity, and death has been noted often.[13] Moreover, syntactic slippage within this discourse enacts a fusion of identity whereby Agnes is named by David as simultaneously his 'sweet sister', his 'better angel', and the 'perfect likeness' of her own dead mother (229). Narrative discourse also facilitates a slippage of identity between Agnes and David's own dead mother in the associative displacement of saintly stained-glass imagery onto the iconographic last glimpse David has of his mother, perfectly still, holding her baby in her arms. This primary image which evokes the desired return to mother/child unity is re-presented in the account of Agnes's role at Dora's death. 'When the Angel of Death alighted ... my child-wife fell asleep ... on her bosom with a smile' (659). The ambiguity of the pronoun 'her' marks the associative slippage between Agnes and the Angel of Death. When David is united with Agnes, the currents of desire traversing the narrative culminate in the stasis of death. In this consummation all the sliding identities of the text — mother/wife/child — are pulled into a regressive, narcissistic unity. As David looks into the 'true eyes' of Agnes, 'the spirit of my child-wife looked upon me', while in that glance 'toiling on, I saw a ragged way-worn boy forsaken and neglected, who should come to call even the heart now beating against mine his own' (739). The apparent narrative progress of heroic self-construction has in fact only enacted a compulsive circling back upon erasure of identity in death.

This 'bourne' of the narrative, like the myth of moral progress, seems inimical to a convincing construction of the hero as creative writer. In the kingdom of art no less than in heaven the greatest may be those who remain as little children, but not in a regressive desire for total quiescence. Art requires active transformation – an encoding within the Symbolic of primary experience as 'pleasure, freshness and gentleness', as well as registering the anguish of their loss. These are the feminine qualities which David, interpellated as 'Daisy', represents for Steerforth; a feminine version of self remaining in touch with that pre-Oedipal world of 'dreams and shadows'. Elsewhere in the text these qualities are materialized in the sexually attractive, but vulnerable and victimized female characters. The text synchronizes the beginning of the career as writer with the beginning of the love for Dora – according to Freud both sexual and creative impulses are manifestations of the same life instincts. Despite this, narrative discourse is punitive in its attitude to Dora's spirit of playfulness and her resistance to the repressive morality of order, punctuality and discipline. It seems possible that by means of fictional representation the text is articulating an anxiety Dickens himself felt about feminine aspects of his own creative energy. The sense of otherness, an inheritance of the pre-Oedipal unity with the mother, is essential for the active transformational process of imaginative art. Yet it would seem to threaten disintegration of the unitary social self, and especially of a self constructed so assertively masculine and patriarchal as that of Dickens. Hence the fictional representation of femininity in *David Copperfield* evokes in the text a response of male repression and destruction.

The other area of repression enacted in narrative discourse is that knowledge of 'London life and London streets' deemed so shameful to the genteel self interpellated as 'Trotwood'. Yet this experience, like that of infancy, is related deliberately to the capacity for creative transformation. The adult narrator breaks into narrative representation of early life to explain that the details of his youthful experience with Micawber and the debtors' prison are given to demonstrate how '[I] made stories for myself out of the streets, and out of men and women; and how some main points in the character I shall unconsciously develop, I suppose, in writing my life, were gradually forming all this while' (144). The word 'unconscious' here is revealing. As we have seen, two of the main functions of narrative discourse are the willed construction of moral hero as gentleman. The discourse of class differentiation strives continually to separate David from the world of the streets, out of which menacing characters materialize like a repressed unconscious. The 'innocent romantic boy, making his imagination out of such strange experiences and sordid things' is a self split off and repressed after the retreat from London streets, just as Dickens himself split off and repressed from his public image the self who had experience the raw vitality of London life. The otherness of class, part of the impulse of the life instincts for union and community, was a source of creative energy for Dickens as writer. However, fear of merging identity with 'common companions' in 'unmerited degradation' made conscious knowledge of this otherness shameful. Like acknowledging femininity, it threatened to disintegrate the socially constructed identity of the writer-hero as gentleman.

The historian Geoffrey Best asks in *Mid-Victorian Britain 1851–70* (1979): 'What penalties of social isolation were paid by those who "rose" from the earthy comradeship of the respectable backstreets to the prim privacies of the genteel suburb?'[14] The text of *David Copperfield* confesses to the potential loss of creative energies as part of the penalty involved in this form of genteel aspiration. As this quotation from Best suggests, *David Copperfield* is more than a displaced psychological representation of its writer's personal anxiety. The narrative construction of David as moral hero and gentleman provides an imaginary resolution of the competing ideologies of gentility and progress in a struggle for hegemonic dominance between capitalist and aristocratic interests taking place at the end of the 1840s. It is a resolution articulated in other texts comprising the heteroglossia of the era. Typical of the shift in emphasis is a biography in the *Methodist Magazine* which begins with the usual praise for its subject's 'diligent application and persevering industry' leading to the usual worldly success and affluence. However, in what follows an additional note is struck: 'He was always attentive to business and active in it, affable, and, in a proper sense, gentlemanly in his demeanour and conversation' (1847, p. 940).

Where *Copperfield* differs from most of the other texts engaged in this ideological discourse, is that as in all of Dickens's novels, a dialogic, alienated viewpoint is constructed by the narrative which simultaneously unmasks those very ideals the text appears to validate and offer for reader identification. The heroes of David's life whose values are internalized so that he 'turns out' in their images are revealed as identical in their will to power and repression, despite external differences of manner. The gentlemanly Steerforth is shown to be as brutal as either Murdstone or Creakle, and it is his discourse, especially, which images the most callous class oppression. All three of these characters exhibit the sadism which Freud saw as a manifestation of the death instincts projected outwards upon the world. Furthermore, at a deeper narrative level the text traces the retreat from life and progressive social energy entailed in the gentlemanly ideal. The desire for gentility masks the desire for quiescence and death. So, by the 1850s, began a slow ebbing away of energy and life force within British culture, disguised but not checked by the rise of empire.

However, fulfilment of the confessional impulse implicit in the novel's first sentence extends beyond this deconstruction of heroic status. What the text confesses to, most poignantly, is the inability to disengage imaginative desire from the romantic Absolute Subject signified in the social encodement of 'gentleman'. Despite the unveiling of a pernicious reality underlying the myth, David's love for Steerforth, even after the seduction of Em'ly and destruction of the Yarmouth home, is the most strongly registered desire of the text. Thus what is ultimately 'confessed' by the novel is the betrayal of an oppositional ideal to that of gentility – the utopian glimpse offered at the beginning in Daniel Peggotty's material transformation of loss into community. That glimpse remains sealed off in the Imaginary; the Peggottys are never represented, as Sam Weller and Sairey Gamp are, within a specific social world. The last years of the 1840s saw the end of a period of intense, striving social energies and ideological struggle. Out of some part of these fluxing energies a transformational ideal of equality, community, and co-operation was constructed. In the event, the dominant class forces of individualism and capitalism prevailed and in the hegemonic ascendancy consolidated thereafter, a radical, utopian, alternative concept of 'progress' was repressed and sealed off to remain only a haunting, unrealizable dream.

Notes

1. R. K. Webb, p. 248.
2. For an account of this, see Harold Perkins, p. 412–13.
3. Dickens offers a highly satiric description of this 'wonderful hybrid' match in *Hard Times* (1854), II.2.
4. Martin J. Weiner, *English Culture and the Decline of the Industrial Spirit 1850–1980* (1982), p. 14.
5. Quoted in Weiner, p. 33.
6. Weiner, pp. 5–6.
7. This social class division of maternal image and role was, of course, an

actual one for most middle-class children who were cared for largely by working-class women as wet nurses, nannies, etc.

8. *Methodist Magazine*, (1848), pp. 626–7. A list of title headings gives some sense of the repressiveness of this discourse: 'Family Government', 'Rewards and Punishments', 'Spiritual Strength as a Duty', Submission to God', 'Duty of Self-Communion', 'Manner in which Trials and Afflictions should be borne'. This last-named article outlines the problem which is central to *Copperfield*: that of a man who 'meet[s] no sympathy where he would most fondly seek it: [no] companionship with those of his own household'. Such a situation is to be seen as a 'painful discipline' calling the individual 'to discover the duty to which it points' (*Christian Observer*, 1848, pp. 249–50).

9. Angus Wilson, *The World of Charles Dickens* (Harmondsworth, Middlesex, 1972), p. 216.

10. The most straightforward expression of this idea is probably Julia Kristeva's statement: 'I think that every type of creation, even if it's scientific, is due to this possibility of opening the norms, towards pleasure, which refers to an archaic experience with a maternal pre-object.' 'A Question of Subjectivity' *Women's Review*, 12 (1986), p. 20. For a fuller discussion see also 'Revolution in Poetic Language' in *The Kristeva Reader*, edited by Toril Moi (1986), p. 113.

11. Freud, *Beyond the Pleasure Principle* in the Pelican Freud Library, Vol. 11 (1984), pp. 311, 336.

12. Pelican Freud Library, Vol. 11, p. 313.

13. See, for example, the discussion by Alexander Welsh, *The City of Dickens* (1971), pp. 180–3.

14. Geoffrey Best, p. 310.

4

Bleak House:
Alienated Readers

The cluster of threatening events in 1848 – cholera, revolutions in Europe, and Chartism at home – and their seemingly miraculous dispersal without dire consequences gave rise, in England at the turn of the decade, to a hegemonic discourse upon the ways of Divine Providence. It was a discourse characterized by congratulatory complacency. Great Britain, it seemed evident, was under a special dispensation. 'Old England,' rejoiced the *Methodist Magazine*, in 1849, 'has never looked so fair in the eyes of her children as during the last twelve months. While her neighbour kingdoms of Europe have been prostrated, or writhing, she has been sitting hale and serene ... "God has been on our side" now may England say' (1849, p. 509). Internal tranquillity was not the only blessing bestowed upon the nation by an approving hand of Providence. The expansion of trade and empire were seen also as part of a divinely appointed national destiny: 'England is called to be the light of the nations. ... The time of our manhood is nigh. ... Happy the land which becomes the teacher and Apostle of all humanity!' (1849, pp. 510–11). On the eve of the Great Exhibition, the *Westminster Review*, too, though in more befittingly sober prose, congratulated the country on its ascendancy among nations, taking 'the lead in peace, as she did in war' (53 (1850), p. 90).

This hegemonic discourse of the nation as singled out for God's special favour fostered and justified an intransigent satisfaction with the state of the country's existing institutions and social welfare. The *Christian Observer* printed articles claiming divine precedence and blessing for inequality: 'It is obvious that a law of superiority and subjection prevails through all the dispensations of God. There are archangels as well as angels ... There are kings and subjects – the rich and the poor ... how important is the lesson conveyed by this law of the Great Ruler of the universe – to the inferior classes of creation – that subjection which we are tempted at first sight to regard as an evil, may be – and is calculated to be – a blessing' (1851, p. 221). In *Bleak*

House, the character discourse of Sir Leicester Dedlock, who believes that the 'slow, expensive, British, constitutional kind of thing' including the hereditary power of his own class, has been devised 'for the eternal settlement . . . of everything' (13), materializes the speech image of this conservative inertia.

The emphasis on subjection in the quotation above from the *Christian Observer* points to the ideology functioning beneath the enthusiasm for Divine Providence in hegemonic discourse. It was aimed at securing submission to the existing dispensations of wealth and power against that disaffected tendency of the times, characterized by Sir Leicester within the text of *Bleak House*, as 'Wat Tylerish'. To quarrel with the 'eternal settlement' was to quarrel with the will of God, who had designed the whole as a vast interlocking causal mechanism; a role indicated in evangelical journals by favoured designations like the First Cause, the Great Conductor of affairs, the Divine Economist, and the Divine Author. In keeping with ideas of a global national destiny, the hegemonic discourse on Providence constructed a sense of lofty panoramic overview of time and space which was consistently opposed to the restricted scope of individual human vision. Apparent injustices or suffering caused by the arrangement of the universe could then be seen as resulting from the incompleteness of human vision unable to comprehend the harmonious interconnection of the whole. Mere human 'worms', warned *Methodist Magazine*, 'see but pieces of the works of God, both as to their extent and duration. As all the letters make one word, and all the words make one sentence, and all the sentences and sections and chapters do make one book – and the use of the letters, syllables, words and sentences cannot be rightly understood and valued if taken separately from the whole, – no more can we rightly understand and value the works of God when we see not their relation to the whole' (1850, p. 130).

This analogy with reading as the connection of individual signs into a totalized order of meaning was the recurring master trope underpinning the discourse on Divine Providence. It was a wholly appropriate image during a period of intense debate about the need to provide basic education for the illiterate and 'godless' working-class poor. In being taught to read their letters it was taken as axiomatic that they should be taught simultaneously to read their place as divinely settled for the course of human history. 'Teach him that God, not man, assigned his lot and you will have taught him that which alone can be depended upon to make him respectful and contented,' wrote *Christian Observer* (1852, p. 155).

The duty to read social ordering and national history in terms of a vast cosmic system of interconnected cause and effect was continually stressed in dominant Providential discourse. 'All the connexions of things' were 'many parts of the economic policy of Jehovah,' showing that 'one infinite Mind planned the work,' explained the *Methodist Magazine* (1850, pp. 1279–80). Or, using a more literary image, the history of the race was a 'Divine plot, a wide-spread and long-acted drama ... spread over all the world, and over all time' (1850, p. 242). The bible was the 'one great education' needed to teach the correct method of reading the Divine design behind human history. Rather as in a detective novel, sign must be connected to sign to reveal plot: 'Through the connexions which these writings [Scriptures] afford, and the hidden parts of the history which they disclose, strange events are accounted for ... untoward occurrences are now seen to form parts of a well-ordered and benevolent plan' (1850, p. 140).

In contrast to the difficulty in comprehending this Divine plan in its universal and cosmic scale, the causal plot imposing retrospective meaning upon individual lives was available for all to read. This was because the Great Ruler of the universe maintained a minute-by-minute scrutiny of every deed and thought of each of his creatures, subjecting them to a continual process of judgement, retribution or reward. Inner grace or guilt were signified to all in the signs of worldly well-being. Thus small as well as large misfortunes and prosperities could be read retrospectively as divine approbation or punishment for past acts of righteousness or sin. Chadband's character discourse offers a representation of this prevailing moral economy in which a mishap or reversal was balanced as payment to the 'Divine debt collector' against an earlier misdemeanour: 'It is right that I should be corrected. I stumbled, on Sabbath last ... The account is now favourably balanced: my creditor has accepted a composition' (270). Such meticulous spiritual accountancy provided a pleasing sense of moral solvency, but material prosperity too was a sign to be read as righteousness rewarded. The purified heart might well 'qualify for the safe enjoyment of a greater amount of temporal prosperity' wrote the *Methodist Magazine* (1850, p. 834).

This reading of worldly signs to signify an inner state of guilt or grace provided a comfortable sense of self-approbation for those materially able to exhibit 'godly' signs. For those who could not, however, to be read was to be interpellated into a damning system of meaning. When a 'drunken wretch' was burnt to death in a house fire the incident was 'read' by a correspondent to *Methodist Magazine* as the judgement of God confirming and punishing past wickedness: 'Righteous art Thou O Lord, and just art Thy judgements,' concluded the writer (1851, p. 529). The working class generally, just like Jo the crossing-sweeper in his 'unwholesome rags', were read without hesitation as 'graceless creature[s]' (149); the inexorable connection between material signifier and spiritual signified bonded by that single term 'graceless'. Reviewing Mayhew's *London Labour and London Poor*, the *Christian Observer* warned against forgetting the 'immutable connection between vice and misery' (1852, p. 234). The Victorian poor, therefore, were trapped within two orders of reading, both of which inculcated a sense of fatalism and subjection. On the one hand, they were exhorted to read their proper place as a pre-ordained link within the vast eternally settled design of Divine Providence. On the other hand, they were interpellated into a system of meaning which read their particular individual lives in terms of guilt and divine disapprobation. 'If there is a God,' wrote the *Methodist Magazine*, 'there must be a universal monarchy and an absolute regent will. Subjection — physical, political, moral — must therefore be the philosophy of human life' (1850, p. 243). But it was essentially the subjection of the working class that this discourse of an eternally ordered and individually punishing Providence was designed to secure.

Despite the surface complacency engendered by this discourse on Providential settlement, there were points of fracture and contradiction which became the focus of nagging social anxiety. This unease was caused by a suppressed realization that the separation of classes was neither so absolute nor so eternally fixed as dominant discourse attempted to maintain. There was hidden perception that the respectable classes and the labouring poor were intimately and causally linked in such a way as to bring about just that 'confusion' and 'obliteration' of boundaries feared by Sir Leicester in *Bleak House*. The extreme poverty of the working class rendered them a persistent source of contagious diseases; more scandalously, the starvation wages of working-class women, in particular, enforced a continuous supply of purchasable sex for middle-class men outwith the sanctity of the bourgeois home.

These perceptions and the fears they aroused focussed upon the accelerating rate of juvenile crime associated with a growing number of illegitimate and orphaned children,[1] and it was expressed frequently in imagery of proliferating disease. The *Methodist Magazine* noted that the cholera epidemics had resulted in large numbers of orphans 'cast upon the public care and the public purse' (1850, p. 246). In 1851, the *Westminster Review* reported that on average there would be about

40,000 pauper children in the union workhouses of England and Wales and a large proportion of these would be orphans (55 (1851), p. 456). These parentless children would grow up struggling for existence in the anarchic environment of the city streets, untouched by any teaching, any social connection, or any fostering care. To the respectable they seemed 'a nation within a nation', a shifting tribe of 'semi-savages' in their midst with no 'proper place' allotted them. In an article on 'Juvenile Delinquency', the *Methodist Magazine* wrote of the 'frightful' figures of youthful crime as a 'symptom of a disease' in which each delinquent was a centre of spreading 'infection' undermining social order (1852, p. 44).

It was difficult to read this increase in the number of children without any proper place in the world as part of Providential design. There was an even more embarrassed silence upon the main cause of illegitimate infants – the vast resort to prostitution by Victorian men. However, the *Westminster Review* was less coy, insisting that prostitution was the 'gangrene' of society and continuing this imagery of pervasive infection throughout the article (53 (1850), pp. 474–7). With 50,000 prostitutes spreading syphilitic disease through all classes and into unborn generations, precautions against cholera seemed beside the point, wrote the reviewer. According to the journal not one man in ten went through life without being infected at some time. Such scandalous interconnection of classes was not to be read as part of a harmonious order, but rather detection of such connection was the shadow of disgrace haunting many respectable families, as in *Bleak House*, it haunts Mrs Snagsby's suspicions of her husband's parental connection with Jo. 'On this topic,' wrote the *Westminster*, 'some frightful disclosures have from time to time to be hushed up' (53 (1850), p. 476). The text of *Bleak House*, therefore, with its large number of abandoned children, its imagery of disease, and its threats of sexual scandal in high places is probing at the most sensitive fears of social disintegration of its era. The interconnected malaise of poverty, prostitution, disease, illegitimacy, and juvenile crime was undoubtedly the 'Tough Subject' of the early 1850s, insinuating a threat of seeping disintegration throughout the social fabric.

In the 1850s, the *Westminster Review* continued to uphold the myth of the guilty poor, insisting that the main causes of poverty were 'indolence, unskilfulness, extravagance, drunkenness, dishonesty, and unpunctuality' (52 (1849), p. 92). However, it had also become increasingly indignant at government complacency, and accordingly appropriated the persuasive power of Providential discourse to articulate its demand for political change. 'Would cholera and plague in an ill-drained town be characterized a dispensation of Providence?' it demanded ironically (52 (1849), p. 94). The *Westminster* further heightened the urgency of such questions by fusing references to Providence with an apocalyptic rhetoric and tone. Referring to the late revolution in France it declared, 'We seem to have stood as witness to the opening of the seventh seal . . . and the words that rise to our lips are those of the Apocalypse . . . "thus with violence shall Babylon be cast down" ' (49 (1848), pp. 137–8). From 1848–1851, the *Westminster* continued in this vein, using similar apocalyptic language to draw warning parallels between the corrupt government of Louis-Philippe, toppled like a 'rotten tree', and the political intransigence and time-serving at home. References to the Book of Revelations were a familiar characteristic of Chartist and socialist oratory, and so the *Westminster* was playing knowingly upon public fears that the 'semi-savages' might not always subject themselves tamely to the will of Providence, but instead seize a proper and better place for themselves. Thus readers were invited to speculate on the 'wolfish physiognomies' of the vagrant poor and imagine London in the hands 'for three days of such sections of our population' (50 (1849), p. 193). According to this view, the poor became signifiers within yet another order of meaning. They were to be read as signs of imminent social revolution; a violent 'moral earthquake' necessary to sweep away the intransigence of the privileged and one which 'must therefore be accepted, with other calamities, as a law of Providence' (50 (1849), p. 193).

Bleak House is centrally concerned with the ideological subjection of subjects and positions itself dialogically in the midst of the conflicts articulated within Providential discourse. Moreover, the narrative division is structured upon that opposition between the cosmic perspective available to a Supreme Being (the Divine Author?) and the restricted viewpoint of an individual creature. The internal past-tense narrative of Esther provides a retrospective reading of the signs inscribing the causal plot of her particular life – a life bound within the specific, observable time-scale of individual history. However, the voice of the external narrator should be read also as mimetic representation. It materializes a Providential viewpoint which exists in an eternal present and is cognisant with all dimensions of time and space. It is this impersonal narrative voice, rather than that of a working-class character, which is the locus of a pervasive ironic anger and a comic parodic impulse to unveil and mock oppressive power. The scale of temporal reference in the text is befittingly vast, moving easily from the antediluvian forests of Dedlock timber to the dying fires of the sun. As this suggests, the whole of the solar system provides the order within which to read the importance of the British ruling class, and the irony is cosmic: 'The fashionable world – tremendous orb, nearly five miles round – is in full swing, and the solar system works respectfully at its appointed distances' (650). This shifting ironic focus from the diastolic to the systolic, from panoramic sweep to close-up intensity, characterizes the external narrator's providential viewpoint. Textual references to Quebec, Malta, Africa, and India map out the scale of British dominion, but narrative scrutiny returns insistently to the 'home-grown' filth and misery of Tom-all-Alone's. The narrator's estimate of national greatness is encompassed in a single epithet 'this boastful island' – the noun contemptuously emphasized in antithesis to inflated views of national destiny (151).

Like the 'Divine Author' or 'Great Ruler of the Universe', the external narrator exercises total power over his creatures: narrative discourse brings the portraits of dead Dedlocks briefly to life so that 'a staring Baronet . . . gets a dimple in his chin . . . [and] a maid of honour . . . seems to bathe in glowing water'. But in the next paragraph the narrative voice reconsigns these newly-resurrected Dedlocks to 'age and death' (563–4). However, unlike the judgemental God of the Chadbands and of Esther's godmother, who visits the sins of the parents upon their children, the voice of the external narrator is never harsh or vengeful. The narrator's judgements – slyly ironic in revealing the pompous anachronism of Sir Leicester Dedlock, ominous in juxtaposing the Roman with the British empire, outraged at the death of Jo – construct a sustained oppositional voice to that of hegemonic Providential discourse. While this latter evokes an inexorable, punishing Jehovah, the external narrative expresses a passionate, involved concern with suffering and injustice.[2]

This ironic, dialogic interaction of the discourse of the external narrator with dominant discourse is intensified by the richly heteroglot quality of the narrative voice. Apart from the tremendous emotional range imaged by this voice (in contrast to the unitary tonality of dominant discourse) it constructs a densely interwoven verbal texture of allusions, reference, mimicry, and parodic appropriation. One major chain of intertextual allusion embedded in the narrative is to Matthew 25 – a text itself engaging in multiple ways with Providential discourse in the parables of the Wise Virgins and the Last Judgement. This latter parable made uncomfortable reading for evangelicals and for the wealthy by its insistence that sheep shall be separated from goats for eternal salvation or damnation, not in accordance with election, but according to the material compassion shown to fellow beings in this world – feeding the hungry and tending the sick. In *Bleak House* it is largely the poor, outcast, and despised who are represented as so doing, and with sly humour narrative discourse consistently refers to the poor as sheep and lambs, while pointing out that lawyers all have wigs of goat hair![3]

The need for timely preparation against the Last Day embodied in the story of the Wise Virgins interconnects with multiple textual images and references playing upon oppositional concepts of time and judgement: individual time-span against the inertia of law, history against eternity, urgent present against distant past and future. These are articulated in allusion to fairy-tale (Sleeping Beauty, for example), parody of political and legal rhetoric, references to classical history, and to recent events of the French Revolution. However, the most pervasive chain of intertextual association is to the Book of Revelations with its apocalyptic warnings of the destruction of 'the kings of the earth, and the great men, and the rich men', whilst the poor 'shall hunger no more, neither thirst any more . . . and God shall wipe away all tears from their eyes' (6.14; 7.14–17). The main function of this whole network of allusion is an extended parodic mockery of the reactionary complacency of power in Britain at the opening of the 1850s, by means of a comic subversion of the hegemonic discourses of Providence, classical antiquity, and statesmanship. However, given the incipient fears of plague, social disintegration, and revolt, the narrative appropriation of apocalyptic imagery insinuates a chilling threat of serious possibility.

In keeping with the parodic representation of a Providential viewpoint, the external narrator is omniscient, but not all-revealing. Indeed, the reader is interpellated into a text where teasing hints and suggested mysteries are used deliberately as strategies to provoke a reading practice which looks consciously for signs and connections out of which to construct a plot. John Forster commented upon the exceptionally careful causal plotting of *Bleak House*, where nothing is 'random', where 'event leads more closely to event' and every part of the story is linked to 'one strong chain'.[4] However, as the reader actively connects sign to sign to construct the whole system of meaning, what is unveiled at every point is the human causation and human plotters hiding behind 'providential' kinds of explanation. Just as Guster's fits are not signs of divine wrath, but of physical brutality inflicted by an all-too-human patron saint at the Tooting orphanage, so all the suffering and misery represented in the text is depicted as stemming directly from human agency. The imagery describing Tom-all-Alone's is infernal, but it is a man-made hell and the poor are shown to be punished not by God, but by class laws and political neglect. Neither is it God who visits the sins of her parents upon the orphaned Charley Neckett, but those, like the Smallweeds, who exploit the unpopularity of her father's calling to pay her an even lower rate. The magistrate's court purports to express divine judgement on Jo, putting him 'aside' as 'terribly depraved' (148). However, it is officers of the law, like Bucket, and members of the respectable classes, like Mrs Snagsby, whom the text depicts as harassing him to the point of death.

Law is represented in the text as at the centre of this proliferating system of misreading, subsuming all other structures of mystification. This is wholly appropriate, since law is the ultimate foundation and guarantor of the existing 'providential' dispensations of property, privilege, and power. Moreover, law is the formal institution for defining what is guilt and what is innocence, what is legitimate and what illegitimate. In *Bleak House*, the imposition of a sense of guilt and illegitimacy – in the widest sense of having no right to exist – is unveiled as the mechanism of submission, constructing subjects who 'willingly' subject themselves to subjection.

Thus, while the reader of the text is encouraged to join word to word to construct the plot of a vast interconnected system of injustice and victimization, an objective diastolic perspective, the victims within the text are represented as trapped in and by words. Social orders of discourse imaged in the text are shown to be used, like the legal rhetoric of Kenge, to construct mystifying systems of meaning which sustain the structure of power and 'consolidate it for a thousand ages' (844). To enter the Symbolic Order – to read – is thus to be pulled into the partial systolic view of reality offered by ideological structures. Characters interpellated into these systems are positioned within an order of meaning which they cannot fully read or control. They are denied objective knowledge of causation, knowing only their place within the whole. Thus Mr Snagsby allows himself to be interpellated by Bucket: 'You're a man of the world . . . That's what *you* are' (308). As a result, he is entangled in a mysterious chain of signs and events which he cannot link together – read – as a coherent system of meaning, but within which he feels obscurely and submissively that he must be guilty in some way: 'His mental sufferings are so great, that he entertains wandering ideas of delivering himself up to justice, and requiring to be cleared if innocent, and punished with the utmost rigour of the law, if guilty' (461).

Snagsby's case is mirrored in the representation of other victimized characters. All are marked by a sense of powerlessness, fatalism, and guilt. They 'know their place' within a larger order of meaning, but lack the objective diastolic perspective of the external narrator, and offered the reader, to comprehend the whole. Similarly, Esther is represented in her sick dream as praying for relief but as unable to escape from her place in the chain. Caught up into these mystifying systems of discourse, all these characters are represented as submitting themselves to the treatment they feel they must deserve. Caddy and Prince Turveydrop are interpellated into the order of Deportment, in the signs of which they read their own inferior position and duty to work. Miss Flite's sense of the terrible and mystical power of Law, reified in its symbols of Mace and Seal, positions her in total subjection to its authority. These victims are represented as regarding the source of their oppression with 'deference', 'veneration', and 'pride' (192). All of them are like Miss Flite in exhibiting that simultaneous combination of desire for identification along with a self-denigrating recognition of lack and distance which characterizes the interpellation of subject to Absolute Subject, margin to centre, thus ensuring the willing subjection of subjects.

Krook's inability to read: 'He knows most of [the letters] separately, ... but he cannot put them together' (450), is reminiscent of the human ignorance of divine causation described in the *Methodist Magazine*, as an inability to connect letter to letter to construct the whole. However, given the guilt and submission induced in those who are interpellated into systolic systems of meaning, Krook's suspicious refusal to be taught by anyone 'because they might teach me wrong' comes to seem a wily strategy of self-preservation (201).

The detailed functioning of this repressive mechanism of reading is set out in the text through two related case studies of individual marginalization: the particular histories of Esther and Jo. Even before their structural interlinking in disease, these two character representations are implicitly connected by shameful birth: both are termed 'destitute' subjects and 'set apart' (18, 22). However, like David Copperfield, Esther has a double function in the text as both a character and a narrator; her confessional discourse, too, is marked by an ambiguous duplicity. In order, therefore, to read the full implications of Esther's place within the total signifying system of *Bleak House*, it is necessary to interrelate the psychological presentation of her as character with the problematic status of her narrative.

An understanding of the presentation of Esther as character is aided by reinserting her discourse into the order of meaning in which it originates. Her speech image reproduces the tone and characteristics of the confessional discourse found in the self-scrutinizing spiritual diaries, extracted and printed in most issues of the *Methodist Magazine*. This form of confessional writing seems to have been much practised by women, and its emphasis on self-criticism promoted a morbid probing of motivation and recurring expressions of self-doubt and unworthiness – precisely those aspects of Esther's discourse which evoke modern reader resistance. One typical diary extract begins, 'Help me, Lord, to be upright and truly sincere in thus noting down my feelings and desires. I would not hide the stirrings of my evil propensities' (1849, p. 788). 'I shall not conceal as I go,' promises Esther's narrative, 'the weaknesses I could not quite conquer' (505). Prominent within these personal biographies of pious women was an emphasis upon virtuous domesticity, seeming frequently to go along with a repressive insistence upon self-denial and sin. Many, like this extract printed in 1852, are reminiscent of Esther's industrious Dame Durden image: 'Her management of her house was worthy of a woman professing godliness. Diligent, punctual, energetic, she allowed no room for the intrusion of sloth or disorder within the range of her domestic authority and influence' (1852, p. 1055). However, often it is the moral rigidity of Esther's godmother which is brought to mind: 'She imposed on herself, even to the end of her life, a system of rigid economy and self-denial, which, if detailed, would seem scarcely credible ... and her children were taught ... that it is a sin to be idle' (1851, p. 532).[5] Unattractive though some of this writing is, it must have provided countless women with justification for writing about their feelings and their lives. In the pages of *Methodist Magazine* many otherwise unknown and unimportant women found their own experience and their own words validated in print. The confessional form of these writings offered a licence to speak to those whose discourse was otherwise excluded from the public domain.

Nevertheless, confession of guilt was the price exacted for this entry into the realm of social discourse. The climax to which every biographical account moved was the admission of sin. Semantic duality nicely points up the conditions of possibility governing this discourse: to *admit* guilt was the necessary price of *admission* into the society of the elect. It is in keeping with its confessional form, therefore, that Esther's personal narrative opens with an admission of her own inadequacy and is regularly interspersed with conciliatory disclaimers of any personal merit. Esther, as character, is represented as only too willing to pay the coin of entry into social discourse, since she is inscribed with an even darker sense of sin than normal. 'You are different from other children, Esther, because you were not born, like them, in common sinfulness and wrath. You are set apart,' her godmother has told her (18). Thus Esther's earliest sense of self-identity is represented as founded upon the experience of marginalization and lack. She knows herself through difference. She is different from everyone she meets, but most different of all from the person who is at the centre of her childhood world and who wields total power over it: her *god-mother*. For Esther this figure engenders a double force of desire; she represents the lost mother and the ego-ideal of an Imaginary, beautiful, angelic, and justified self. However, her godmother seems to Esther like an angel who frowns, the image of displeased divinity, and the sense of distance Esther feels between herself and this desired ego-ideal measures her own hopeless sense of lack – 'so poor, so trifling, and so far off' (15).

Like the other victimized characters represented in the text, Esther is denied any objective knowledge of the origins of her guilt and outcast position, although like them she feels she 'should like to understand it better' (15). This need to relate meaningfully to the social world in which she finds herself, to know her place within it, makes Esther more than willing to pay the price of admission into social community. She resolves submissively to 'try as hard as ever I could, to repair the fault I had been born with (of which I confessedly felt guilty and yet innocent)' and strive to be 'industrious, contented, and kind-hearted' in the hope of winning 'some love to myself if I could' (18). From thence onwards, in a manner similar to Chadband's moral accountancy, Esther's discourse tabulates an emotional credit account morbidly registering every sign which she may read as an indication that she is indeed loved – that her existence in the world is legitimate and justified.

Esther represents how as a child she fashioned for herself a less forbidding and less distant ego-ideal than that of her godmother for reflecting back a desired self. The doll with the 'beautiful complexion and rosy lips' subsumes both the need for a lovable self-identity and for a loving mother (15). In adulthood, Esther as character, is represented as finding a life-size doll in Ada, whose name functions as a displaced echo of her own. Ada's outward smiling beauty can be read as a reliable signifier of a loving angelic inner nature – she is the angel who smiles. The insistent possessive pronouns which characterize

Esther's interpellation of Ada as 'my pet', 'my darling' indicates narcissistic desire for identification with this ideal. The representation of Esther's ambiguous feelings towards Ada produces the only current of sexual energy in the text, climaxing, almost literally, in the intensely charged depiction of the reunion between the two women after Esther's illness and disfigurement. It is this reunion, rather than that with the actual lost mother, Lady Dedlock, which is shot through with the passionate emotion of a consummation with the object of desire. Esther's obsession with her physical appearance should not be read as signifying vanity, but of unappeasable anxiety about her own inner worth. The scarring with smallpox, therefore, was a sign to be read by her as a visitation of the old disapproving divinity of her childhood, marking her outwardly with the signifiers of a sinful and ugly inner nature. The meeting with her real mother serves only to reinforce this sense of what the evangelicals called 'the sad heirloom of sin' whereby the guilt of parents was perpetuated in their children. Coming immediately after this meeting with her mother, the interchangeable language of Esther's and Ada's reunion – 'my darling', 'my dear', 'my love', 'my angel girl', 'my sweet beautiful girl', 'rocking me to and fro like a child' – enacts a narcissistic slippage between all the relations of desire (517). Lover, mother, child, and self, Esther identifies herself with all of these in Ada.

Considered as a narration – as the totalizing meaning which Esther as character reads back into her own life – her story clearly functions to construct an image of the desired Imaginary self. Like many of the writers of the autobiographical extracts in the *Methodist Magazine*, Esther's narrative discourse exploits the licence offered by the confessional form to covertly catalogue moral virtue while proclaiming humility. Her retrospectively organized personal history, culminating in the happy domestic ending, constructs a causal moral plot in which her original inner virtue is recognized and rewarded at last, and Esther assigned her proper place at the very centre of that little adoring company of the elect at Bleak House.[6] This is the fairy-tale hinted at when she compared herself to a princess in a story book at the outset of her narrative. Esther has transformed herself into the object of desire, an Absolute Subject with the power to interpellate others into conformity with her idealized image. As a construct of her own reading, she signifies a promise to others of what her godmother demanded of her: 'Submission, self-denial' and 'industrious content-ment'; these are the admission price of social acceptance and love. This materialization of her own childhood need of a desirable, justified identity, achieved through narrative reconstruction of her life, brackets off Esther's story within the text of *Bleak House* as wish-fulfilment or as an Imaginary ideological 'solution', and this is how we, as external readers, should read all the elements within it. How comforting it would be if everything did turn out well in the end, if individual goodness could prevail – as in the consoling world of Providential discourse.

But to read social experience in such a way is wilfully to mystify perception and turn a blind eye to the interconnection of power and subjection. Readers of *Bleak House* are interpellated into a diastolic overview which denies the consolation of such restricted vision through the dialogic interaction of the two narratives. John Jarndice's individual benevolence has to be read from the same ironic perspective that mocks the futility of Mr Snagsby's 'infallible remedy' of half-a-crown offered as 'magic balm' to staunch all social ills (646). The hegemonic myth of individual moral worth, inevitably redeemed and recognized in worldly prosperity, validated in the causal plot of Esther's narrative (but undermined in the complex psychological representation of her as character) is challenged and subverted by the external narrative, and especially by the particular history embedded within it of the orphan Jo.

Jo the crossing-sweeper is one of a series of similar representations within both Dickens's short stories and his longer fiction. They are characters, who, like Nancy in *Oliver Twist*, Maypole Hugh in *Barnaby Rudge*, Magwitch in *Great Expectations*, and the wolfish boys in *Christmas Carol* and *Haunted Man*, have been orphaned and abandoned in their earliest years and left to struggle for a precarious existence on the city streets. However, these 'young Cains' are represented without the sharpness of a Sam Weller or the social drive of a David Copperfield; their 'progress' in the texts inevitably traces a downward path, usually towards early death. Their most overt ideological function in the fiction is to serve as warnings to the respectable classes of the dangers inherent in neglecting the city poor. 'Beware this boy', says the ghost of Christmas Present to Scrooge. However, usually these characters are constructed also as moral examples whose impulses of fellowship are intended to shame the self-interest and greed of the well-to-do in the real world. Maypole Hugh is typical of this dual functioning, threatening those who use him ill that 'my bark is nothing to my bite' (304). However, while the law callously sentences Barnaby Rudge to death, Hugh treats him with gentleness and compassion.

The representation of Jo conforms to this double pattern. Jo is compared unfavourably with a trained sheep dog, and, warns the narrator, 'Turn that dog's descendents wild, like Jo, and in a very few years they will so degenerate that they will lose even their bark – but not their bite' (222). The centrality of this warning to the whole novel is underlined by its use as illustration for the title page of the first edition.[7] Despite this, and despite the law's verdict on him as 'terribly depraved', it is Jo who sweeps the steps of the scandalous graveyard in an act of fellowship with Nemo, buried there by his more respectable *fellow*men.

Unlike Esther, though, there is no fairy-tale element of transformation in Jo's story. His inner moral worth is not finally recognized and rewarded in outward material forms. Jo is not a prince in disguise as in story books; neither can he fulfil the reactionary Puseyite romanticism of Sir Leicester's class who construct a wishfulfilling fantasy of a feudal poor, 'very picturesque and faithful' (160).[8] Jo, and his like in the real streets, have not even the glamour of exotic distance and race. The voice of the external narrator is insistently anti-Romantic in cataloguing the mundane physical nastiness of Jo's condition: 'Dirty, ugly, disagreeable to all the senses ... Homely filth begrimes him, homely parasites devour him, homely sores are in him, homely rags are on him: native ignorance, the growth of English soil and climate, sinks his immortal nature lower than the beasts that perish' (641).

In 1850 the *Westminster Review* discussed a series of articles on the 'state of England' appearing in the *Morning Chronicle*, *The Times*, and the *Edinburgh Review* in response to the 'terror' evoked by the late cholera epidemic. Summing up the scale of 'homely' squalor, misery, and destitution revealed in these journals, the *Westminster*'s reviewer concluded that it was such as to make 'high-spirited men wonder how there could be so much tame submission, and the thoughtful to be a little anxious lest this tameness of submission should come to an end' (53 (1850), p. 145). The representation of Jo, read in conjunction with the characterization of Esther, unveils the means by which such inexplicable submissiveness in the poor was maintained.

At the beginning of his particular story within the external narrative, Jo is represented as totally orphaned, having no connection at all to the social community: 'No father, no mother, no friend', and the tenuous link with Nemo (no-one) ended in the latter's death. The Court of Justice in putting him aside merely gives the seal of legal sanction to a verdict already enacted by society. The existence of those like Jo, designated in the text 'the outlaw' and 'the outcast' (219, 647), is judged illegitimate in all ways. Bucket, ubiquitous agent of the law, spells it out in words which even an illiterate can understand, 'Hook it, nobody wants you here' (634). Jo's condition is represented as one of perpetual 'moving on' because he belongs nowhere; he cannot know or find his proper place because he has 'no business here, or there, or anywhere' (221). As such, his very existence in the world is unjustified, his simply being anywhere a cause of guilt. The slum, Tom-all-Alone's, where he and other outcasts and outlaws crowd for shelter resembles a real hell in that it defines those wretched enough to live there as 'cut off from honest company and put out of the pale of hope' (220). Its name 'all-Alone's' names also their illegitimate condition in the world – their loss of all social connection.

In 1849, the *Christian Observer* noted in alarm that 'Vagrancy is now becoming the character of our common people . . . a mass which rolls over the surface of the country . . . Knowing no-one, respecting no-one, loving no-one' (1849, pp. 82–3). Such is the representation of Jo as completely outside the social community. It would be misleading to designate Jo as a marginalized character, since even that extremity implies a relationship of some kind with the centre. Jo's inability to read his letters represents complete estrangement from the Symbolic order. None of its structuring systems of signs conveys any meaning or offers any position to him at all.

'It must be a strange state to be like Jo', suggests the external narrator, nudging the reader of those words towards empathetic speculation. To be like Jo is to be strange to self. A sense of self-identity can only be constructed in conjunction with a sense of others. 'I' can only evolve from a meaningful opposition to 'you'. Jo is represented as too distanced from other people fully to construct a sense of self identity out of his relation to them. He can 'no-think' self. The frequent use of the third person singular form in the construction of Jo's speech image in the early stage of his presentation functions to convey this lack of interiority: 'Can't exactly say what'll be done to him arter he's dead if he tells a lie to the gentlemen here, but believes it'll be something wery bad to punish him, and serve him right' (148). Esther's narrative describes him as 'strangely unconcerned about himself', and again the epithet emphasizes his self-estrangement (433). But there are advantages in such a state of unselfconsciousness. Unable to read himself into any meaningful place in the social order, Jo is unburdened by comparative notions of his own worth. His discourse, and especially his answers to questions about himself are characterized by dispassionate impersonality – strangely unconcerned about himself

– and an absence of shame. To contrast Jo's speech pattern in the early part of his presentation with Esther's guilt-saturated discourse is to perceive that lack of self-awareness offers a form of freedom from internalized social constraints. This disconnection from the social community protects Jo from interpellation by Chadband and other religious missionaries to the poor. To Jo they seemed only to be 'a-talking to theirselves' (648). This has positive benefits. A visitor to a ragged school wrote enthusiastically to the *Methodist Magazine*: 'I found them well versed in the doctrine of original sin. From scripture they proved that man *was born* sinful' (1850, p. 854).

In the early part of Jo's history in the text, the only utterances within his discourse which convey some sense of inner consciousness relate to his connection with Nemo – 'He was wery good to me' (149). From this brief experience of community a soberly ironic causal chain is constructed which brings Jo into closer and closer connection with the social world of the respectable – he begins to find a place. Fittingly, the first stage of this structural movement into community is concluded when fellow-orphan Guster is represented as patting him gently on the shoulder, 'the first time in his life that any decent hand has been so laid upon him' (362). The second stage is initiated by the compassion of another orphan, Charley Neckett, bringing him into connection with Esther and her circle. The final phase depicts him nursed by a third orphan, Phil Quod. The discourse of all three of these parentless characters is dominated by a fervent gratitude to those perceived as having provided them with a 'place'[9] – a sense of justified existence and social identity. This need for social connection is a pressing one, and these three orphans are represented as 'freely' anxious to serve those who appear to provide it for them.

As Jo becomes linked into a meaningful relationship with the respectable – as he enters the social order – so the representation of his speech and thoughts conveys the construction of subjectivity. However, as with the representation of Esther in her childhood, it is self-perception founded upon such an extreme of difference that inevitably with it there comes a sense of lack and shame: 'He seems to know that they have an inclination to shrink from him ... He too shrinks from them. He is not of the same order of things, not of the same place of creation' (641). As Jo learns to read the place allotted him, what he learns simultaneously is his own undesirability.

In any social formation structured upon competitive inequality, the interpellation of margin to centre inevitably imposes just such a perception of hopeless lack in those at the margin. For the 'graceless' poor, without possessions, position, or status, their distance from any image of desire can only be read by them as the measure of their own unworth. Their very place in the social structure signifies, like living at Tom-all-Alone's, the original guilt of birth. The diastolic perspective offered the reader of Jo's story within the external narrative reveals a collective political guilt of neglect and victimization. However, Jo as character is shown to 'read' his personal history in terms of self-blame, seeking to justify his existence by reparation. Having discovered at last the power of signifying systems, Jo is eager to pay the *admission* fee for a place within social discourse. Like Esther he is ready and willing to confess. He commissions Mr Snagsby to 'write out, wery large so that any one could see it anywheres, as that I was wery truly hearty sorry that I done it' (647). The chapter is entitled 'Jo's Will', and this is his bequest. It is the only thing society does not begrudge the poor: a willed and willing moral guilt. Thus with ironic inevitability it is Jo, who, on entering the social community, catches its most pernicious infection. It is the infection of shame, imposed with the inequality of class, and ensuring the willing subjection of the poor in perpetuity.

Notes

1. Such was public anxiety that a £100 prize was offered for the best essay on this subject (*Westminster Review*, 52 (1850), p. 589).
2. It was not just evangelicals who conjured a punishing Providence against the working class. The discourse of political economy could be strikingly similar. The *Edinburgh Review* propounded a rigid economic morality, declaring that to relieve those who were destitute through their own or their parents' fault was to go against the 'laws of nature and of Providence'. For those who are 'destitute by their parents' culpability ... the sins of the fathers are visited upon the children ... let us not lose sight of the indubitable truth that ... if we intercede the penalty ... we perpetuate the sin' (90 (1849), p. 512). Even the *Westminster Review* felt moved to protest against this harsh application of Utilitarian principles.
3. See, for example, pp. 2, 311, 640, 663.
4. John Forster, *Life of Charles Dickens*, edited by A. J. Hoppe, 2 vols (1966), II, 114.
5. As with these last two quotations, often the personal journal extracts were used within a longer laudatory biography written by a son or husband of the deceased woman.
6. The title given to the first chapter of Esther's story, 'A Progress', foreshadows this plot of moral progress which will structure her narrative.

7. The iconography of Jo's broom and its interrelation with the apocalyptic imagery may have been more accessible to nineteenth-century readers. In *Lark Rise to Candleford*, Flora Thompson describes a fiery itinerant preacher whose text was 'I will sweep them off the face of the earth with the besom of destruction' (Harmondsworth, Middlesex, 1973, p. 218).

8. Butt and Tillotson, *Dickens at Work* (1957), drew attention to the satiric portrayal of Puseyites in *Bleak House*, as well as its attack upon Chancery and government inertia (pp. 117–200).

9. It is difficult now to re-articulate the whole lived structure of power and subordination condensed into this one word within Victorian class discourse. The need to ask for a 'place' provides a stark reminder of the sufferance upon which the working class were allotted an existence.

Part III:
Containment of Discontent

5

Great Expectations: A Bought Self

Perhaps the most striking feature of public discourse in the late 1850s and early 1860s was the virtual disappearance of anxiety about the working class. Up to that time the labouring poor featured continually within dominant discourse as a perceived source of menace to the moral, economic, social, and physical well-being of the nation. In the journals of 1859 and 1860 a silence seems to have fallen upon the problem of the poor – a silence strikingly acknowledged in *The Times*: 'We are all glad not to hear the long loud wail of the poor' (25 June 1860).

The late 1850s and early 1860s have been seen as the golden age of Victorian England, an epithet utilized at the time: 'In spite of rail, and steam, and machinery ours is even more a golden than an *iron* age' *The Times* wrote (26 July 1860). In the same year the *Christian Observer* remarked that, 'At home we enjoy profound repose. England was never so great, yet never was she governed with so much ease; never did she exhibit, in all classes, so much contentment' (1860, p. 797). Nothing illustrated this climate of 'contentment' so clearly as the lack of interest in the proposal before Parliament for further electoral reform. Whereas in 1832 the subject was charged with passion and violence, the reaction recorded in all the journals was summed up by *The Times*: 'All classes have resolved to treat the subject as unimportant because they are tired of it' (1 March 1860). In its 'Retrospect of the Year 1859' the *Christian Observer* concluded that 'the experience of every year confirms and extends the conviction in all classes that the English constitution . . . is still the best . . . the world has ever seen . . . The wildest reformers never venture to hint at a democracy' (1860, p. 69). Within this dominant discourse of contentment, which characterized the age, the representation of class relations underwent a change from imagery stressing opposition and difference to that of association and linkage. Instead of reiterating the irredeemable separation of the working class from the ideal

103

of respectability, public pronouncements began to assert their assimilation to this desired image. The eighteenth-century notion of society as a ladder or chain of connection was rediscovered.[1] The *Christian Observer* wrote of the nation as 'one great family' (1860, p. 710); the *Edinburgh Review* declared that 'the different classes of society are more firmly knit together' (109 (1859), p. 282); while the *Westminster Review* argued in favour of 'nicely-shaded social relations and inter-woven charities of life' (71 (1859), p. 151).

The title of 'golden age' for this era is appropriate in yet another way. Replacing anxiety about the state of the poor, the major topic of dominant discourse at this time was concern with wealth and its conspicuous display. Throughout 1859 and 1860 evangelical journals printed sermon upon sermon deprecating 'the feverish endeavour after the accumulation of wealth' (*Methodist Magazine*, 1859, p. 401). This theme was echoed in the *Westminster Review*: 'intense desire for wealth,' wrote a reviewer, was due to the 'indiscriminate respect' paid to affluence and riches so that 'wealth and respectability [have become] two sides of the same thing' (71 (1859), p. 385). Within this discourse upon wealth the words 'fashionable' and 'worldly' constantly recurred; it was the life-style and outward spectacle of wealth that fascinated and were desired. 'Wealth is one of the most attractive "fashions" that the world assumes,' wrote the *Methodist Magazine*, 'it dazzles with its brightness' (1859, pp. 600–1). The *Christian Observer* described the 'Perils of the Present Day' as 'the fashionable dress, the late hour, the luxurious display' (1859, pp. 219–20). Not surprisingly, this attraction towards the outward style and symbolism of wealth corresponded with a renewed popularity of royalty and the aristocracy. However, this was less a reverence for the mystique of birth than the more modern desire to participate vicariously in the glamour which nobility symbolized. This is what Bagehot, writing at the time, called 'the theatrical show of society . . . a certain spectacle of beautiful women; a wonderful scene of wealth . . . [a] charmed spectacle which imposes on the many and guides their fancies as it will'.[2] Bagehot pointed to this admiring identification of the mass in the glamour of the few as explanation for the absence of political discontent in England. His view was endorsed in the *Edinburgh Review*; the working classes, it wrote, were not tempted by republicanism or socialism, 'they love the monarchy, they take pride in the aristocracy' (112 (1860), p. 291). A letter to *The Times* declared it was the duty of government to maintain this high position of the aristocracy in the people's esteem, and it was signed in ostentatious deference, 'A Common Fellow' (11 February 1860).

This fantasy identification with the spectacle of wealth and nobility was aided, during these 'golden' middle years of the century, by widespread dissemination of the myth of individual success. If society was indeed a chain of connection, everyone could aspire to reach its heights. The *Methodist Magazine* asserted in 1859 that the 'inevitable circumstances of birth [and] early life' have little effect upon a man's destiny. 'Loneliness and insignificance' were barriers to be 'beaten down' by 'a strong will and hand' on the 'upward progress to wealth and fame'. Echoing further the imagery in *Great Expectations*, the journal warned that those who fail in this path to success were usually those who had themselves 'woven' the chains of 'entanglement' (1859, p. 427). The following year the *Christian Observer* drew attention to 'the fashion of late years, especially with our public lecturers' of holding out the 'golden image' of success to young men as in the keeping of their own will to achieve it. This 'sentiment has been, within the last few years, a hundred times repeated' (1860, p. 352). It was the *Westminster Review* which most fully explored the social implications of the continuous reiteration of this 'golden image' of success and the resulting identification of wealth with respectability. From earliest years, wrote the reviewer, a poor boy has it 'burnt into his memory that poverty is contemptible' so that before long the desire for wealth becomes an 'organic conviction'. But, according to the reviewer, this desire was not so much for wealth itself, as for its outward spectacle, 'the applause and position which [it] brings' (71 (1859), p. 385).

Undoubtedly, throughout the 1850s and 1860s the wealth of the middle class increased spectacularly and this allowed them to purchase a life-style of conspicuous luxurious display. But, as the quotations above suggest, this period also marks the initial moment of that long wooing of the working class with the dream of a consumerist life-style; a shift from inhibiting interpellation in terms of lack and guilt, to interpellation as promise. In reality, though, this consumer dream, the 'golden image' of wealthy style, remained only a fairytale for all but a very small proportion of the working class. Social mobility actually decreased after 1850, and the huge increase in national prosperity barely trickled down to the working class at all in the fifties and sixties. Furthermore, the emphasis on fashionable style and consumer display, far from creating any genuine national unity of 'contentment', actually functioned to create ever-finer nuances of social distinction and division. Stark class boundaries (and therefore class solidarity) were conveniently blurred by this increasing consumerism, but, wrote the *Westminster Review* astutely, 'by the accumulation of wealth, by style, by beauty of dress . . . each tries to subjugate others, and so aids in weaving that ramified network of restraints by which society is kept in order' (72 (1859), p. 3). Even in dominant discourse like this the ambivalence of the recurring chain/weaving trope points to the duplicity of the hegemonic myth of society as a benevolent chain of connection. Chains more frequently hold things in place.

The dark side of the 'feverish endeavour after wealth' and pressure for conspicuous display was an increasing interconnection of money with crime, especially crimes of greed, malpractice, and business fraud. 'If anyone would obtain a key to the forms of English life in the year 1860,' wrote *The Times,* 'he would do well to read carefully from day to day the records of conflicting interest and crime' (5 April 1860). A few months before this a leading article characterized the age as one in which 'corruptions are bubbling up to the surface every hour' (5 January 1860). The *Westminster Review* also confirmed this view, suggesting that endemic crime, especially commercial malpractice, was a 'gigantic system of dishonesty . . . [with] roots which run underneath our whole social fabric' (71 (1859), pp. 386–7). Public perception of a criminal underside to wealth disturbed that ideological construction of a golden haze of general prosperity interweaving the whole nation into unified contentment. However, what posed the greatest threat to this hegemonic fairytale was the continuing poverty of large numbers of the working class, for whom belief in the 'golden image' of success could prove a cruelly mocking enchantment. 'In the most brilliant thoroughfares of modern London we brush against human beings whose life is one long martydom,' wrote *The Times.* Frequently these were those 'whom the real or imaginary wealth of London and the innumerable openings it is supposed to present to enterprise have allured away from home' (24 December 1860). The solution to this inconvenient problem of continuing destitution, which challenged the hegemonic culture of contentment and enterprise, was to exclude it from public notice and consideration. Ironically, in view of the increase in crimes of greed, it was the poor who were constructed as criminalized.

The process of exclusion and containment of the working class poor was much aided by the increasing separation of classes, as the well-to-do retreated to fashionable suburbs away from 'the annoyance of the crowded city' (*Christian Observer,* 1859, p. 487). This growing trend was commented upon frequently in the journals of the early 1860s, and this comfortable residential seclusion allowed uncomfortable facts about the labour which produced both the wealth and the items of its display to be forgotten. In 1860 the *Westminster Review* printed a long article detailing the terrible injuries and debilitation suffered by those employed in luxury trades; it pointed out that although the wealthy 'have never given a thought' to the manner in which its wants are supplied, yet 'every article of luxury' in their drawing-rooms 'would disclose to us pictures of workmen transiently or permanently disabled in the production of them' (111 (1860), pp. 2–3). *The Times*, too, on Christmas Eve, sought to remind its prosperous readers of the real interweaving of their wellbeing with the 'class created, as it were, for our convenience'. Fashionable demand was locked into a causal chain with poverty. *The Times*' writer continued, 'few are aware how large a proportion of those who minister to our daily wants and comfort are liable to be thrown out of employment by a very slight oscillation in the balance of supply and demand... disturbances of the labour market, we are told, right themselves in time, but meanwhile flesh and blood have succumbed and men and women have been starved or reduced to beggary' (24 December 1860).

The grim reality of this chain of interconnection, which produced, out of sheer necessity of life, a ready supply of workers for poisonous trades was ignored within the myth of national contentment. This ignorance of the real conditions of labour facilitated the rewriting of the working-class poor as a semi-criminalized sub-class of those too dishonest or lazy to will their own success. This myth was strengthened by a glowing report in 1860 on the working of the Poor Laws which claimed that pauperism (the dependency culture) had been eradicated at a saving of over £33 million to ratepayers. Within this euphemistic discourse, the favoured term for the poor became 'the residuum', with the consoling implication that the main problem of class poverty was resolved.

In effect, by criminalizing and shaming poverty the Poor Laws had merely taught it to hide its face. 'While we are all glad not to hear the long loud wail of the poor,' wrote *The Times*, in response to the Poor Law Report, 'much is done that is never known' (25 June 1860). In the House of Lords, Lord Shaftesbury spoke of 'the many unhappy beings [who] are so filthy and ill-clad that they are ashamed to come out into the light and expose themselves to the public gaze. They creep forth under the shadow and shelter of night' (*Christian Observer*, 1859, p. 278). In addition to internalized shame, improved surveillance methods also kept poverty out of sight and perceived as criminalized. Earlier in the century, troops and force were the only means of reacting to social unrest. By the 1850s, the police force had sufficient numbers and efficiency to maintain a perpetual watchfulness on behalf of the propertied. If the presence of the poor attracted attention, a police officer would inevitably appear to disperse them. Mayhew wrote bitterly of the 'aristocratic pride of the commercial classes' in utilizing the police to force street people continually to 'move on' (II, 3). This repression of the reality of poverty from the knowledge and experience of prosperous life led to the erosion of outrage. The problem of class poverty and its discontent had not been solved, but it had been silenced – pushed out of sight and out of mind.

Dialogic engagement with the hegemonic golden images of success, wealth, and contentment, and their silenced reverse of poverty and crime, is displaced into the wholly appropriate fairytale form of *Great Expectations*. Clearly this novel constructs a parodic fable aimed at an ironic exposure of national enchantment with the myth of great expectations for all. The narrative not only unmasks the interconnection of money, crime, and power hiding beneath glamorous spectacle, but also it stages a scandalous return of the repressed and criminalized poor. However, fairytale is a rich, archaic form, closely associated with rituals of transformation and with symbolic figuration of desire, and these traditions remain active in the text, adding a polysemic complexity to its exploration of aspiration and social identity. The radical contentiousness of the novel is disguised by backdating the story to earlier in the century, although Herbert's search for a career opening in shipping insurance situates it within the financial and imperial world of the post-1850s. However, this backdating, like the fairytale form, is multiply functional. The earlier period of criminal transportation allows for the dramatic enactment of return. More importantly, it produces an effect of condensation so that synchronic novelistic images articulate the complex process of historical change, whereby control of discontent moved from external force to inner coercion, and then to the persuasive promise of consumer dream. In addition to this, the text seizes dialogically upon the words 'common' and 'fellow' and upon images of connection recurrent in dominant discourse and renders them sites of immediate ideological conflict, to be resaturated with radical intent.[3]

Great Expectations opens with the fictional subject it is to construct first coming to a sense of 'the identity of things' (1). As character, Pip is shown to acquire a perception of self through experienced difference; as a small, sentient, 'bundle of shivers' enacted upon by a hostile physical universe (1). Thus from the first inception of the narrative, Pip is represented as a subjected subject. This is the common inheritance of all creatures, and Pip's shivering flesh underlines his fellowship with 'the terrible man' who had been 'soaked in water...lamed by stones...stung by nettles...who limped and shivered...and whose teeth chattered in his head' (2). It is this bondage to fundamental physical needs of hunger, warmth, and creature contact which inscribes human commonness. By contrast, the main function of socially-created artificial needs is to rewrite this connection, and thereby invest 'commonness' with an opposite derogatory value. Consumer life-styles construct what the *Westminster Review* correctly designated 'a network of restraints' whereby the 'identity of things' becomes caught up in a signifying system of social esteem. Recognition of common need is articulated in young Pip's pity for the convict's 'desolation' and in the discourse of Joe: 'We don't know what you have done, but we wouldn't have you starved to death for it, poor miserable fellow-creatur' (36).

However, in the world represented by the text, subjection to physical force comes largely from fellow human beings. Mimetic representation of Pip's first moment of awareness of self as subject of a physical world, is immediately followed by his brutal subjection to human force. Prior to this he has been subject to his sister's bringing-up by hand and by 'Tickler'. Magwitch, too, is depicted as a creature shackled with the physical chains of oppressive state power, and these chains are used later to subdue and subject Mrs Joe. Bonds of connection binding family or state are unmasked in the text as largely characterized by violence and intimidation, not as ladders to success and prosperity. Smithfield and Newgate lie side by side in the heart of London, mirror-images of each other and reflecting the ultimate manifestation of physical state power: creatures herded out 'to be killed in a row' (156).

However, the efficacy of physical power is limited to its presence. From the eighteenth century onwards, the state came to rely less and less upon terrorizing and punishing the physical body of those resistent to its authority, and more and more upon means of internalizing restraint and fear in those perceived as even potentially discontented. These means can be generalized as the inculcation within the individual subject of a sense of perpetual surveillance. The apparatuses of this subjection were multiple, from incarceration regimes like the Silent System, monitoring systems in education, and the construction of the police force, but undoubtedly the most powerfully dispersed influence was evangelicalism, with its relentless insistence upon inner guilt perceived by an ever-watchful God. The representation of Magwitch provides an illustrative image of this historical transition from external force to inner coercion. In order to retain power over the child Pip when he is no longer present to exert physical terror, Magwitch is forced to invent the young man who has 'a secret way, pecooliar to himself, of getting at a boy, and at his heart, and at his liver. . . . that young man will softly creep and creep his way to him and tear him open' (3–4).

This young man with such terrifying powers of secret access foreshadows the representation of Jaggers, whose total inscrutability, combined with a terrorizing reputation for clairvoyance, constructs him as the very personification of the panoptican State. The depiction of Jaggers's methods reveals the efficacy, in terms of social control, of criminalizing the subject. Jaggers deliberately extends opportunities for petty crime in the way of those perceived as potentially unlawful in order to bring them fully into his control – so that 'he has 'em soul and body' (249). Those brought thus within the system of law become not only subjects to be punished, but also objects of knowledge, individualized and spotlighted within an all-encompassing scrutiny – souls rather than bodies are the object of this power. Magwitch has his head measured as part of this process whereby criminality became an object of knowledge, dispersing and banishing discontent amidst a grid of 'scientific' statistics. Jaggers is represented as taming a 'wild beast' by making her the object of his knowledge, but the power he represents extends beyond those actually guilty of crime. The coercively forensic style of his character discourse persistently insinuates access to guilty personal secrets, and thus imposes self-perception of a guilty, criminal subjectivity upon all those he interpellates. In this way he gains a 'detrimental mastery' over his 'fellow-creatures' (155). Under exposure to the gaze that seems to know 'something secret about everyone', characters are depicted as feeling a compulsion 'freely' to confess inner guilt (128). Asked by Pip what he was 'brought up to be', Magwitch is represented as confessing with alacrity 'A warmint'. He answers truly in that being 'brought up' before the law initiated that process of internalized social control whereby the potentially discontented are constructed as guilty, criminalized subjects.

'Sin and law are things which assume the necessity of each other' asserted the *Methodist Magazine* in an article whose title, 'Conscience in Young People', seems an echo of those meditations upon self-guilt articulated by Pip as narrator. The young person, the journal continued, 'perceives the authority of the "law" within him, and understands the dread tribunal to which conscience manifestly refers'

(1859, pp. 200–2). Evangelical discourse persistently obliterated boundaries between God, state, and parent so that children must have felt themselves bound in every aspect of life within a totalized system of scrutinization and judgement.

In the text of *Great Expectations* the direct and indirect speech images of Mrs Joe's character discourse reproduce this repressive language, constructing around Pip, as child, a similar sense of exacting surveillance of which he is at once the known, judged, and punished subject. This represents Pip's first loss of self, as he is recast – forged – in the language of original sin. He is 'a young offender', his birth an offence committed against 'reason, religion, and morality' and this guilty state is signified by clothes made 'like a kind of Reformatory': a complete fusion of the terminology of sin and crime. Appropriately, therefore, the adult Pip's narrative discourse articulates this internalized guilt by constructing its subject as social sinner. The predominating word within narrative language of self is 'conscience' and the narrative voice constructs a sense of subjectivity burdened with a guilt which seems to well up spontaneously from within in an urgent desire to confess.[4] This distinguishes it sharply from the first person confessional narrative of *David Copperfield*, and this difference registers a difference in class representation. The narrative discourse of the adult Copperfield constructs its subject as hero of moral progress, an ego-ideal of bourgeois individualism. In *Great Expectations*, the adult narrator's self-condemnation articulates the ineradicable social guilt of those born poor.

However, the representation of Pip as character, opened up to desire by Satis House, offers a fictional exploration of the subsequent historical shift in the ideological means of containing discontent away from internalized repression to the promise of plenitude. With the expansion into mass-production capitalism in the second half of the nineteenth century, the interpellative emphasis began to shift from the construction of subjects in terms of inhibiting lack and guilt, to that of promise. Instead of functioning as measure of hopeless distance, desire for an Imaginary ego-ideal was increasingly deflected into a dream of consumer plenitude, thus functioning not only to contain potential discontent, but also to stimulate demand-led economic expansion. When the *Methodist Magazine* drew attention in 1859 to a change in the methods of social control, it referred not to internalized guilt, but to the power of consumer persuasion: 'The world has more effective engines than the rack, and the wheel, and the gibbet; it has pleasures and riches and honours' (1859, p. 31).

At Satis House Pip is shown to catch the 'infection' of social shame (55); in the words of the *Westminster Review* it is 'burnt into his memory that poverty is contemptible'. Significantly, the contempt is attached, from the very start, to attributes of lifestyle, to the thick boots, rough hands, and colloquial speech of 'a common labouring boy' (55) In rejecting the contemptible self-image these attributes signify, there is an awakening of desire for all that is perceived as uncommon: for the glamour, refinement, and exclusivity of Estella as a carefully constructed image of desire. That Pip as character is seduced by a fairytale of wealth is indicated in the images he is represented as inventing, whose function is to mark an absolute separation between the world symbolized by Satis House (a misnaming of plenitude, as Estella reveals, p. 51) and the realities of life, now perceived as fundamentally lacking, at the forge. Coaches, golden dishes, enormous dogs, flags and swords are props from a spectacle of fairytale pomp. They conjure a magic world with Pip as participant in its ceremonies of cake and wine – a phantasy wish-fulfillment engendered by actual experience of distance and exclusion.

Desire for the ideal is an inescapable impulse of human life originating, according to Lacan, in the misrecognition of a phantasy specular ego-ideal. The drive throughout life to rediscover that lost perception of self-plenitude is the unconscious impulse stimulating an inventive urge to transform present actuality; but it is also a discontent easily displaced into the conforming ideals of self valorized and glamourized within social structures. Increasingly this unconscious desire has been captured by the fairytale promises offered in the phantasy glamour and plenitude of consumer style. Within the discourse of Pip as character, the star imagery associated with Estella condenses and contains these oppositional directions of desire. The image of the star and the poetic intensification of language associated with it function in the text to create a felt pulse of yearning desire for a transforming, visionary expansiveness able to transcend the physical and mental confinement of a low horizon. This aspect of the speech image constructed by Pip's character discourse remains always outside the judgemental domain of the narrator's moral discourse and uncontainable by its self-repressing guilt.

However, the star image also embodies the sense of an aloof, glittering social world, tantalizing and glamorous. Its double interpellation of hopeless distance and teasing infatuation is articulated in Pip's explanation of his 'lies': 'She had said I was common ... I knew I was common and ... I wished I was not common' (65). Just as the word 'conscience' is the key signifying term within the moral discourse of the adult narrator, so from this point the word 'common' becomes central and recurrent in the speech image associated with Pip as character. The word functions continually and ironically to separate and reject lifestyles and attributes perceived as contemptible. 'I had believed in the best parlour as a most elegant saloon ... I had believed in the forge as the glowing road to manhood and independence ... Now, it was all coarse and common' (100). Rejection of 'commonness' is represented as leading to loss of connection with that non-hegemonic oppositional sense of 'commonness' inscribed in the opening episodes of the text. Throughout the novel common needs like hunger and clothing are shown as elaborated into uncommon practices of differentiating lifestyle, forming 'networks of restraint' like those depicted inhibiting Joe on the visit to London and indicated by the separating encroachment of 'Sir' into his character discourse. Appropriately the principle of differentiating lifestyle is articulated most explicitly in the character discourse of Estella: 'Since your change of fortune and prospects, you have changed companions ... what was fit company for you once, would be quite unfit company for you now' (223). Acceptance of these social rules governing degrees of connectedness is represented mimetically in Pip's increased tendency to use money rather than personal contact as the currency of human relations. This retreat from connection with the reality of other lives – from commonness – is shown to lead to the erosion of compassion. Pip's first reaction to Newgate on arrival in London is represented as one of outrage and horror. Later, having been conducted inside by Wemmick, his response is depicted as having changed to that of abhorrence at his own contamination with its reality. The speech image of Pip as child to the convict articulates pitying fellow-feeling, the character discourse of Pip as gentleman expresses the will for disconnection: 'I cannot wish to renew that chance intercourse with you of long ago ... our ways are different ways' (301).

Narrative construction of Pip as gentleman reveals that more is lost in the materialization of that fairytale 'golden image' of wealth than connection with the lives of others. It represents a second loss – or forging – of self. Pip is shown to mark his changed expectations by a metamorphosis of self-image. He orders himself a 'fashionable suit of clothes', 'an article much in vogue among the nobility and gentry' (143). So he begins to construct the appropriate style of wealth. Indeed, the only employment of Pip as gentleman offered by the narrative account is that of conspicuous consumption and display. The studies with Mr Pocket are never detailed, but reader attention is frequently called to descriptions of lifestyle. His rooms are luxuriously furnished, his personal appearance enhanced by jewellery, his status advertized by the canary livery of the Avenger, and his reputation confirmed by membership of a fashionable club. Pip as character is shown to become a gentleman by assuming the style of wealth. This is probably the first representation of the yuppy in fiction. What this constructs is a life of surface, a consumerist perception of self as bought. The dialogic challenge to this within the text is Wemmick's inventive pleasure in a self-made domestic lifestyle whose gadgets are all intended to enhance connection by breaching the Aged's isolating deafness. 'I am my own engineer, and my own plumber, and my own gardener' he is presented as telling Pip (196).

In Pip's case, even the bought style is based upon growing debts, and this in turn is based upon false expectations. The whole existence as gentleman is represented in the text as a falsification and a counterfeiting of self. The fairytale form of transformation into prince reverses over into the curse of stolen or enchanted identity. The adult narrator names himself with the deep bitterness of loss a 'self-swindler', cheating himself with 'spurious coin' of his own making (213). There is a sad diminishment in the movement of the narrative from that initial fairytale invocation of transformation and celebration in terms of golden dishes and velvet coaches to the representation of Pip's empty pretence of plenitude in London, that 'gay fiction among us that we were all constantly enjoying ourselves, and a skeleton truth that we never did' (260). Despite its fictionality the process of genteel restyling is depicted as devoid of imagination. Pip's capacity for playfulness died at Satis House. The text presents his transformation into gentleman as merely a matter of buying the appropriate style of display. Nothing could be more different from the inventive and opportunist process of continuous self-making represented in the street characters of Dickens's earliest texts. Sam Weller's theatrical performance of self constitutes a celebration of superfluity in common life, refusing the low horizon of an existence bounded by mere necessity. Its spectacle is inclusive, irradiating participants with shared glamour in a spirit of playful transformation. By contrast the spectacle of wealthy style as presented in Pip as character is intended to intimidate those it separates off as 'common', and it counterfeits self in a bought image. As gentleman, Pip fully reveals that to 'Hav-is-sham'. This falsification of self is appropriately articulated in the parodic mirroring of Pip's pretensions by Trabb's boy, a wonderful re-invention of the urchin: 'Don't know yah, don't know yah, pon my soul don't know yah!' (232).

This imagery of shamming, counterfeiting, or forging is the master trope of the text, locking together the interconnection of money with criminality. Almost all the crime mentioned in the story is of coining, forging, or swindling. Jaggers is even said to keep a smelter on the premises. The whole system of law, as represented in the novel, is implicated in a pervasive network of counterfeiting. Witnesses are paid to 'sham' respectability, innocence is bought from the lawyer best able to construct its appearance. Underlying this forgery of justice by money, is subservience to style. The *Westminster Review*, in writing about the 'gigantic system of dishonesty' running beneath 'our whole social fabric', concluded, 'we are all implicated ... Scarcely a man is to be found who would not behave with more civility to a knave in broadcloth than to a knave in fustian' (71 (1859), p. 387). The account of Magwitch's trial provides a fictional exposure of this use of money to construct the style of respectability and lawfulness.

In 1860, *The Times* described the plight of children orphaned or 'turned out of doors [to] become what are called Arabs of the streets. They have not a hope or a thought but of mendicacy or robbery ... in the streets, in the school of crime, and on the way to prison, or the penal settlement' (15 August 1860). This is a real-life version of the fictional story of Magwitch: 'In jail and out of jail ... carted here and carted there ... tramping, begging, thieving, working sometimes when I could' (329). In the speech image of Magwitch the text constructs a powerful and passionate voice to represent the silenced and criminalized poor. In opposition to the exclusion of poverty from hegemonic discourse of national contentment, Magwitch's character discourse is dominated by an urge for reconnection. While the speech image of Pip as gentleman struggles to defend a sense of separation and differentiation, Magwitch's reiterated interpellation of him as 'dear boy' seeks to pull him into a recognition of affection and intimacy – a 'commonness' which he dreads. The representation of Magwitch's physical gestures, too, stress the impulse to make fellowship material in actual bodily contact. In detailing Pip's shuddering reaction, narrative discourse most powerfully recreates the repugnance and shrinking of the prosperous from the physical reality of those Lord Shaftesbury described as so 'filthy' and 'ill-clad' that they only 'creep forth' at night. The representation of the fairytale sham of fashionable style is shattered by dialogic contact with the intensity conveyed of Magwitch as a physical bodily presence – this is a triumph of the novel's mimetic realism. Once returned, the immediacy and passion of this physical challenge to a counterfeit reality can no longer be pushed from consciousness: 'everything in him that it was most desirable to repress, started through that thin layer of pretence, and seemed to come blazing out at the crown of his head' (319). The energy of the verbs here seems to deny the possibility of any further containment.

However, Magwitch, too, is represented as having bought the consumer dream. His discourse lovingly recognizes and catalogues the items of Pip's fashionable lifestyle: lodgings 'fit for a lord', gold and diamond rings, fine linen, books (305). But Magwitch's discourse overtly connects this consumer desire to the lack which makes its idealized images so impelling to the poor and outcast – the need to escape from a self-image perceived as low or contemptible. 'And then, dear boy, it was a recompense to me, look'ee here, to know in secret that I was making a gentleman' (306). Even a vicarious investment in wealthy style offers defence in phantasy against interpellation as an 'ignorant common fellow', as Bagehot recognized when he described the 'charmed spectacle of society' as 'imposing on the many and guiding their fancies as it will'. Royalty, joined now by various 'stars', constructed, like Estella, as objects of desire, offer that same vicarious and consoling identification with glamour to those unlikely ever to share it, articulated in the character discourse of Magwitch. More importantly, his speech reconnects wealthy lifestyle and conspicuous consumption to the reality of their source in degraded and punishing labour. 'I lived rough, that you should live smooth, I worked hard, that you should be above work' (304). Those words, in their starkness, lay bare the exploitative chain of connection structuring the economic inequality of class. This is always the uncomfortable truth repressed and excluded from the fascinating spectacle of wealth.

Pip, like the prosperous in the real world, is represented as inscribing the space of this repressed knowledge with criminality: 'In the dreadful mystery that he was to me . . . I would sit and look at him, wondering what he had done, and loading him with all the crimes in the Calendar' (319). Pip even mimics the urge to incarcerate the poor, locking Magwitch into his room at night. However, the text does not sanction this recontainment. Magwitch's first person account of his life constructs the criminalized poor, not as object of knowledge, but as passionately knowing subject whose discourse reconnects the link between common needs and 'crimes' of want. While the new discourse of science was elaborating a mystifying typology of criminality constructed upon irrelevant statistical measurements, the language of

Magwitch, in *Great Expectations*, asserts the simple compulsion of hunger: 'What the Devil was I to do? I must put something into my stomach, mustn't I?' (328). The laws of property cannot bind those denied work, food, and shelter. In addition, Magwitch's discourse functions to expose the chain of connection between crimes of need and crimes of greed. Even a slight disturbance of the labour market, *The Times* disclosed, could reduce men and women to starvation and beggary. This level of common need pushed the poor, like Magwitch, into the power of those, like Compeyson, involved in crimes of swindling and fraud, not in order to stay alive, but to indulge the cultivated needs of wealthy lifestyle. The chains of social inter-connection as represented in *Great Expectations* are altogether more harsh and sinister than those presented in the hegemonic myth of 'interwoven charities of life'.

The character discourse of Magwitch is represented as the means of reconnecting Pip with origins in commonness. This narrative pattern of circular return is so obsessive in the later novels of Dickens that the repetition must articulate a desire which refuses containment. Readings which recontain the strong impulse of desire inscribed in the text of *Great Expectations* usually do so by imposing the hegemonic myth of moral progress. Pip's willing public commitment of fellowship to Magwitch is interpreted as the climax of his individual moral regeneration. However, this restriction of the story to the private ignores the deliberately archetypal representation of Magwitch. The name 'Abel' associates him with the first biblical sacrificial prefiguring of Christ; he comes into Pip's life at Christmas and is sentenced to death in April, the season of Easter. Such symbolic dimension is out of proportion to an individualized reading of Pip's story. Clearly, Magwitch is intended to represent the scapegoat poor of prosperous mid-Victorian England, criminalized and punished for the guilt of poverty. As usual, biblical intertextuality opens out the more radical implications of the text. The parable Pip reads to the dying Magwitch is told in Luke 18 as a warning to the wealthy who 'despised others', and it concludes with the words, 'for everyone that exalteth himself shall be abased: and he that humbleth himself shall be exalted'. The chapter then continues with Christ's advice to the wealthy man 'to sell all that thou hast and distribute unto the poor', concluding with a forewarning of how Christ himself will be despised, and beaten, and crucified.

The problem of the two endings to the novel is usually felt to centre upon the disjunction between the narrator Pip and the character Pip:

two subjectivities never fused into a unified individual identity. There is, indeed, a persistent dialogic opposition between the narrative discourse of guilt and the language of desire associated with Pip as character. The first ending is often preferred; its sobriety of tone and the brief meeting and parting of Pip and Estella in London seem more consonant with the modest realism of the moral plot (Pip working hard to repay his debts and earn decent profits), and with the pervasive sense of guilt and loss constructed by the moral discourse of the adult narrator. However, that realism splinters off from the fairytale form of the novel as a whole. Moreover, the self-condemning discourse of the narrative voice, with its urge endlessly to confess, expresses the initial forging of identity into that of sinner. It enacts the repression of desire and its discontent in an inhibiting interpellation of self as guilty.

The fairytale form is used ironically to parody and mock hegemonic promises of prosperous contentment for all. However, fairytale as an archaic form has always functioned to articulate a desire for transformation. The second conclusion articulates the return of that desire. However, it is desire no longer dazzled and bewitched with the promise of exclusive and glamorous style. It reconnects into the imaginative impulse for creative transformation of present low horizons condensed in the star imagery associated with Estella. In this final instance the sense of hopeless distance is evaporated as glittering stars are transposed into tears, a figure of common suffering. The final poetic image of the text, therefore, offers the glimpsed possibility of an oppositional vision of desire as social transformation. Union with Estella as the daughter of Magwitch and Molly is a consummation of commonness, not of differentiating gentility. Together, they are represented walking away from a delusive Eden, shut off from common realities, taking friendship and desire out into the fallen world of work and suffering.

Notes

1. For detailed documentation of this see Asa Briggs' essay, 'The Language of 'Class' in Early Nineteenth-Century England', in *Essays in Labour History*, edited by Asa Briggs and John Saville (1967), pp. 43–73.

2. Quoted in Geoffrey Best, *Mid-Victorian Britain 1851–1870* (1979), p. 259.

3. Dickens entered into this conflict in his current journalism also. Having heard a preacher address a working-class congregation as 'sinners', he wrote passionately, 'Is it not enough to be fellow-creatures, born

yesterday, suffering and striving today, dying tomorrow? By our common capacities for pain and pleasure, by our common laughter and our common tears . . . Surely it is enough to be fellow creatures' ('Two Views of a Cheap Theatre', *All the Year Round*, 25 February, 1860, reprinted in *Uncommercial Traveller*, p. 36.

4. See Michel Foucault, *The History of Sexuality* (1981), p. 60. For an illuminating and detailed reading of *Great Expectations* in relation to Foucault see Jeremy Tambling, 'Prison-bound: Dickens and Foucault', *Essays in Criticism*, 36 (1986), pp. 11–31.

6

Our Mutual Friend: The Taught Self

Somewhere around 1863–4 a moment of hesitation, or of discontent, made itself felt in dominant discourse. As if, after a decade's consolidation of prosperity and hegemonic consensus, there came a doubt as to what actually had been achieved, an intimation of sterility, and a stirring of desire for some new direction, some revitalizing vision beyond the endless pursuit of wealth and self-interest. This ambivalence is articulated frequently in a recurrent trope of the river, in association with a proliferating play upon oppositions of surface and depth, corruption and regeneration, almost as rich in their ramifications as the identical imagery in *Our Mutual Friend*.

There is nothing mysterious about this common choice of language. Not only Darwin's *Origin of Species* (1859), but a continuous stream of archaeological and geological claims, discoveries, books, and lectures created a public consciousness of the evolutionary processes of change, and of the degeneration and regeneration, the 'decline and fall', of civilizations and species. Many of the geological explorations were sited in the mud and dust deposits of river beds and lake shores. In addition to this, public imagination was stirred by the discovery of the source of the Nile in 1862 and by the Suez Canal Project, not completed until 1867. For most Victorians, too, the religious association of Egypt brought readily to mind ideas of bondage, promises of renewal, and birth. The *Methodist Magazine* attacked 'miserable [evolutionary] theories' which would 'lay man lower than the dust' and asked bitterly, 'Are we to be dragged through the slime of Egypt?' (1863, p. 816). In an article celebrating the discovery of the Nile source, *The Times* stressed its revitalizing function as a 'fountain of life' to Egypt (29 November 1862). It needed no great leap of association to link this interest in the Nile to public concern with the Thames, the scandalously polluted state of whose waters and tendency to dangerous flooding were at last being tackled by very extensive embankment and drainage projects. Throughout 1862–3

The Times carried frequent editorial articles upon this work, asserting its necessity, since the poorer population clustering its banks were 'exposed to the evils not only of tide-locked sewers, but of destructive floods. The waters of the Thames burst upon them periodically with the most calamitous effect' (18 January 1862).

The embankment project made the neglected state of the 'teeming populations which lie along the waterside', like those represented in *Our Mutual Friend*, topical during the early 1860s. Unlike the revitalizing mud of the Nile, the polluted flooding of the Thames brought death and endemic disease to these districts. They were focussed upon in the controversial report of the Committee on Education (1861–2)[1] as illustrating the danger of neglecting the education of the poorest sections of the working class: 'the festering soil of these congregated masses *must* be tilled ... if we would not see it covered with such rank growths of vice and crime as would, ere long ... bring us swift and irremediable ruin' (*Christian Observer* (1862), pp. 894–5). This lurid identification of the riverside population with the excremental mud they lived beside, expressed the fears of 'civilized' sections of society that these riverside areas would prove a source of national degeneration and corruption rather than any source of new life. Education was seen as the main evolutionary means of 'cultivating' the 'savagery' of the working-class poor, and the evangelicals were prominent in providing ragged schooling for these poverty-stricken districts. However, the kind of education offered was not intended to stimulate new ideas, let alone generate social change or revitalization. The *Methodist Magazine* declared that education was undertaken 'for the purpose of putting down social disorder and confusion' (1863, p. 256). The evangelicals warned that any attempt to teach the working class the new scientific Darwinian ideas would undermine the authority of religion, that 'only sure bulwark against disaffection and political chaos' (*Methodist Magazine*, 1863, p. 817).

Fears of the degeneration and corruption of national culture also coloured another topical issue of the early 1860s: a concern with what the *Edinburgh Review* called a 'Darwinian competition of languages' (120 (1864), p. 162). There was anxiety that the vulgar speech of the 'uncivilized' and uneducated would defile and overwhelm the purity of 'cultivated' English. Gladstone's abolition of tax on paper in 1861 provoked a noisy public debate. The measure was seen as likely to increase yet further the 'flood' of cheap periodicals and popular newspapers. The evangelicals, in particular were hostile to these as encouraging frivolous and worldly attitudes.[2] In 1863, the *Methodist*

Magazine printed a long article on the dangers of the 'streams of journalism' winding through every street, village, and city 'sometimes sparkling with truth and purity, but more frequently muddy and pestiferous' (1863, p. 1127). Like the analogy of the Harmon murder story ebbing and flowing with the tide, the *Methodist Magazine* saw these journalistic streams as carrying 'gossip to the idle', and spreading a 'banquet of burglaries, suicides and murder before the morbid' – just as the Veneerings and their friends are represented as dining greedily upon their own sensation story. The *Christian Observer* took up the same theme, blaming the 'unhealthy appetite' for sensational stories from the lowest levels of social life for the corruption and degeneration of the English language (1864, p. 614).

These comments formed part of its discussion of Henry Alford's *The Queen's English* which was being extensively reviewed and debated at the time. The *Edinburgh Review* gave extensive coverage to Alford's fears that the 'well of pure sound English' was in 'peril of permanent defilement', setting out his views of a continuous struggle for survival between the purity of the written language of the 'cultivated few' and the spoken language of the 'uncivilized' mass, now being reproduced to provide 'colour' in cheap periodicals (120 (1864), p. 40). However, a reverse form of Darwinian conflict in language had been asserted in a series of popular lectures given by Max Muller at the Royal Institution in 1861, and also discussed at length in the *Edinburgh Review*. For Muller, spoken dialects were 'streams of living speech' flowing beneath and around the 'crystal surface' of literary and cultivated language. This latter had been taken out of 'the living stream of spoken words', lost its 'unbounded capability of change' and become 'artificial'. Muller contended that at times when the higher classes were crushed by social struggles or forced to mix with the lower classes, the 'undercurrent' of vulgar dialect would rise up 'like the waters in spring' to revitalize language and culture (*Edinburgh Review*, 115 (1862), p. 79). Despite the opposite intent of Alford's argument, his conclusions were not so different. A nation whose speech had become 'high-flown and bombastic' must be 'not far from rapid decline, and from being degraded from its former glory' (*Edinburgh Review*, 120 (1864), p. 42).

On the surface of political, social, and religious life in the early 1860s there seemed nothing to indicate any decline from glory. Dominant discourse elaborated a chauvinistic rhetoric of national greatness in which scientific, material, and moral 'progress' were acclaimed as triumphant indications of Britain's evolution into an ever higher scale of civilization. All voices within dominant discourse were united in recognizing the imposing stability and wealth of the nation. The *Methodist Magazine* expressed the consensus view that 'at home there is general prosperity ... Never, perhaps, throughout the country was there more of political quiet and popular content' (1863, p. 1028). The evangelicals had good cause for self-congratulation; their moral sobriety and cult of respectability dominated national culture and professed public values.

Yet despite this, a loss of confidence creeps into their discourse; an anxiety that religious conformism can co-exist comfortably with material corruption and even provide a convenient cover for its existence. The *Christian Observer* admitted, 'The surface of society has of late years been more decent than was perhaps ever known. But the current has been running dark and foul underneath' (1863, p. 801). This article was attacking public complicity with 'vice', especially prostitution, but a frivolous and worldly materialism evinced in obsession with 'amusement' and in increased crime also seemed a symptom of moral degeneration. Thus the journal spoke out against 'expensive habits' of consumption in all classes resulting in increased want of money, so that 'in every walk of life ... malversation, embezzlement, breach of trust, purloining, and even forgery, are becoming matters of everyday occurrence' (1864, p. 242). Such descriptions bring us close to the dishonest pursuit of wealth represented at all social levels in the text of *Our Mutual Friend*.[3] The *Methodist Magazine* wrote in similar vein, acknowledging the 'wide overspreading religiousness of our time', but hinting that this surface veneer cloaked a frivolous materialism and spiritual desuetude (1862, p. 317). In its anxiety over this dislocation of surface profession from inner conviction, the *Methodist Magazine* turned critically upon the hegemonic myths it had fostered and sustained throughout earlier decades of political crisis. The continual lauding of 'self-help', 'self-made men', and 'competition', it complained, fostered hardness of heart in the prosperous. By affirming 'that "if a man does not succeed it is his own fault" ... poverty becomes a species of sin; and it is no great step in advance to treat it as a crime' (1863, pp. 885). Nothing could more surely mark the lessening importance of religion as an ideological apparatus than the willingness to make this admission.

Liberals and Utilitarians also had good reason for contentment. The hegemonic consensus was theirs, with self-interest and the pursuit of wealth everywhere accepted as legitimate motives of desire, and national 'progress' measured solely in terms of these individualistic aspirations. In effect, throughout the early 1860s there was no political opposition. The *Christian Observer* wrote that all the 'great political questions are well-nigh adjusted' (1863, p. 479), while *The Times*, never a friend of Liberalism, admitted that there was not one Conservative politician who could 'pretend that his party has any other policy than to do what the present Ministry has done' (4 February 1862). The Liberal *Edinburgh Review* expressed anxiety lest this 'unanimity' be condemned as 'stagnation', whereas, it asserted, political contentment was a sure sign of an advanced evolutionary state of civilization (117 (1862), pp. 269–271). *The Times*, however, dismissed the early Parliamentary session of 1863 as 'barren' (28 July 1863), and the *Westminster Review* echoed this growing sense of sterility, of Parliament as a political and moral Sahara. 'So barren and wearying a Parliament has not been seen for generations', it wrote, ' . . . a placid, sleek, stultifying kind of self-content [has begun] to steal over the nation'. This 'barrenness' had been brought about by the failure or exhaustion of vision. The Tory party, wrote the reviewer, were without a political creed, whilst Liberalism was the victim of its own success – 'a respectable mediocrity has done it to death' (81 (1864), pp. 124–187).

Below this surface of complacent mediocrity, motivated by money, corruption was rife. 'The plain truth is that any pushing, clever man who has a private interest to serve by entering Parliament . . . can always obtain money', wrote the *Westminster Review* (78 (1862), p. 70), and this resort to bribery and corruption was admitted in all sections of dominant discourse. The *Christian Observer* hoped that Parliament would take steps to purify the Thames, but warned of greater difficulty in cleaning its own House, 'if the waters are foul, the mere turning on of more foul water will not purify the stream' (1862, p. 239). However, as with religion, there was a sharp dislocation between surface profession and underlying intent. Verbally, political corruption, no less than commercial corruption, was condemned on all sides as an intolerable disgrace to national pride, whilst, on all sides, both forms were widespread and intricately interrelated. Veneering was undoubtedly a 'representative man'. Foreigners, wrote *The Times* sarcastically, would think corruption the next worst crime to parricide according to the rhetoric of the House, only to discover outside the House that it was not a crime at all (4 March 1863).

Discontent with the hypocrisy and sterility of dominant culture, with its underside of corruption and greed, articulated within public discourse a current of desire for a regenerating vision. And what that impulse for renewal moved towards, with varying degrees of conscious recognition, was a concept of mutuality, founded in working-class culture. Again the reason for this is not wholly mysterious. 1864 marked the twentieth anniversary of the Rochdale Pioneers and produced a flurry of books on the Co-operative Movement. In reviewing some of these, the *Edinburgh Review* commented upon the increased appreciation the societies had enjoyed of late, with even the ultra-Conservative *Quarterly Review* noticing them favourably. What they have shown, wrote the reviewer, is that 'co-operation may be as productive as competition, whilst . . . as to the moral superiority of the brotherly principle to that of rivalry, there can, we suppose, be no question' (120 (1864), p. 431). Trade unionism was also the subject of several publications and public lectures. In 1861, the *Westminster Review* printed a remarkable essay in which unions were justified as the expression of working-class idealism of which other sections of society now stood in great need. It would be difficult, declared the writer, 'to exaggerate the importance of keeping alive and cultivating that profound social and moral instinct which still exists among the working classes, in spite of all the selfish individualism so sedulously inculcated in them from above' (76 (1861), p. 526). Only among the poor, the article claimed, is the sentiment of fraternity 'not quite extinct', for 'there is in them a deep flow of generous sympathy for their fellow man, which in these latter times is not easily found elsewhere' (76 (1861), p. 542).

The third great force of mutuality constructed out of the privations of working-class life were the friendly societies, which, wrote *The Times*, 'spread underneath the surface of our working-class life like a network of nerves' (5 November 1863). These societies were brought to public attention by the report into their affairs conducted by Mr Tidd Pratt in 1863. *The Times* devoted several lengthy leading articles to them, its tone a comical mixture of admiration and exasperation. 'They have names expressing all imaginable ideas of fellowship and sympathy, but the titles that look like business are relatively rare,' it wrote. The following day it concluded, 'The mischief that is done in commercial companies by dishonesty, is done in these societies by a mis-conception of their duties and objects'. The mistaken duties were later named as 'pity, kind feelings and generosity. We are far from undervaluing these principles . . . but they ought to be kept in their right place' (5, 6, 9 November 1863). Despite which, *The Times* had used its Christmas issue in 1862 to argue that genuine acts of kindness and charity only grew from 'humblest means and opportunities, out of hunger, thirst, nakedness and dear life itself. That, and not the charity of the guinea list, is the only bond to tie the hearts and hands of three million next-door-neighbours' (25 December 1862).[4]

Clearly, the text of *Our Mutual Friend* is intersecting dialogically with dominant 'evolutionary' discourse in its articulation of these issues within public concern. Just as *Bleak House* parodies and unveils the mystifications of a hegemonic discourse upon Providence, so *Our Mutual Friend* constructs a parodic mockery of rhetoric of national progress evinced in a search for origins in dust and mud, and the siting of patriotic pride in the desert of cultural and political life. The nullity of such enterprises is condensed into the imagery of sifting dust heaps; 'There's some things that I never found among the dust' says Boffin (91).[5] The language of the novel plays upon current interest in evolutionary change with characters named as 'brutes' and showing visible signs of degeneration (528, 157, 800). Gaffer and Riderhood barely emerge from the primal slime of the river bed, while Wegg is in mid-process of evolving into insensate woodenness. The final stage of 'civilized' evolution into artificial items of consumption is achieved only in Society; by Twemlow as an 'innocent piece of dinner-furniture', Mrs Podsnap as a magnificent rocking-horse, and the Veneerings smelling 'a little too much of the workshop' – not even honest wood! (6)

As in *Bleak House*, parody in *Our Mutual Friend* is accompanied by anger, but unlike the felt indignation expressed at the plight of Jo the crossing-sweeper, the positive anger articulated around the character of Betty Higden seems somewhat perfunctory.[6] The deeper pulse of anger within the narrative discourse of *Our Mutual Friend* is almost wholly negative; a surge of physical disgust and hatred for the characters represented. This is expressed most clearly in the brutality and violation of the language used: 'you might scalp her, and peel her, and scrape her . . . and yet not penetrate to the genuine article' (119). In a novel about degenerating into savagery, narrative (literary?) language is characterized by a compulsion to slide across boundaries of 'civilized' control.

However, alongside this negative discourse of parody and anger there is articulated an opposing current of positive desire for transformation and resurrection. The picture of the Canterbury pilgrims referred to casually in Chapter Three in fact offers a *mise en abyme* of this central preoccupation of the text. The allusion holds together a fusion of physical and spiritual desire for regeneration which impelled the pilgrims to seek apotheosis after the stagnation and sterility of winter months. This desire is sustained in the references which follow to the Raising of Lazarus and the Deliverance from Egypt (19). These belong to the character discourse of Charley Hexam, who is represented as an evolutionary mixture of 'uncompleted savagery and uncompleted civilization' (18). His desire for individualistic transformation, to 'raise himself in the scale', pressing through into his use of those two biblical illustrations, is echoed in the discourse of many other characters, especially those from the poorer sections of society.[7] Contrary to the views of those like Alford, the impulse for regeneration is represented in the text as at its strongest in those who are culturally and materially most deprived. This desire for some vision beyond the 'one dull enclosure' of poverty is consistently registered and validated in the text (466). It is only the means of escape sought which is subjected to question.

However, narrative discourse, too, is threaded with allusions to the sacraments of burial and baptism, both of which express regeneration of life out of death. Nevertheless, the most persistent marker of desire within narrative language is a recurrent use of 'as if' or 'as though' kinds of formulation. Within narrative discourse, metaphorical descriptions of social conditions in London are closed off as fact by an unqualified use of the verb 'to be'. Thus the Holloway region 'was a tract of suburban Sahara' and 'every street was a sawpit' (33, 144); no linguistic space is allowed for any contention of this grim urban evolution. In contrast to this closed form, the frequent 'as if' formulations connect things *as* they are to an imaginative openness of possibility. When Jenny Wren wants to 'change Is into Was and Was into Is, and keep them so' (435), Riah points out that this change would seal off the possibility of further change, perpetuate her present suffering, and deny the liberating power of 'If' with which they have been comforting themselves. When the meek guest contests Mr Podsnap's denial of starvation, his speech is structured around four emphatic repetitions of 'as if' clauses, used ironically to challenge the closure of Podsnappian certainty with the possibility of a different reality: 'as if starvation had been forced upon the culprits' (140). Within narrative discourse the recurrent use of these formulations is immensely varied.[8] They range from the psychological insight that Jenny Wren's sharp manner 'seemed unavoidable. As if, being turned out in that mould, it must be sharp', to more whimsical descriptions like that of chimney pots fluttering their smoke 'as if they were bridling and fanning themselves' (222, 279). However, the generalized effect of this language pattern is to insinuate into narrative discourse an ever-present possibility of imaginative opening out from the closure of actuality. This transformative impulse is most explicitly articulated in the use of the phrase 'as if' at the end of the passage describing workers leaving the paper mill. In its details, the passage itself seems almost a prevision of William Morris's industrial utopianism. The concluding images are of release and expansion, from the 'rippling circles' in the river to the 'ever-widening beauty of the landscape ... where the sky appeared to meet the earth, as if there were no immensity of space between mankind and Heaven' (689). It is the conjunction of those two small words 'as if' which bridges that space, preventing desire for transformation from floating off into the total escape of a heavenly utopianism. Visionary hopes are retained in a connecting recognition of necessity – of things *as* they are.

John Harmon's discourse also asserts this need to connect imaginative impulses with actuality. Having thought of himself as if he were a ghost among the living, he is represented as saying, 'But this is the fanciful side of the situation. It has a real side ... Don't evade it John Harmon, don't evade it' (366). Undoubtedly, evasion is the defining quality of most character discourse imaged in the text, and almost invariably this involves a corruption or abuse of the inventive play of signifiers: the 'as if' capacity of language. Fictionalization is represented as the prevailing tendency of social discourse. Incidents of human misfortune are dislocated in the sensation press from the actuality of suffering, becoming forms of frivolous entertainment to dispel the prevailing boredom of dinner guests. On the other hand there is a busy fabrication of stories whose function is to gloss over inconvenient facts of poverty and social distress. Such is Fledgeby's 'very convenient fiction' of Riah's secret wealth, and a similar fable about Betty Higden constructs 'a comfortable provision for its subject which costs nobody anything, [thus] this class of fable has long been popular' (278, 504). Literature itself is appropriated in this dislocation of words from actuality. Georgiana Podsnap is shown as persuaded to suspend disbelief in Fledgeby as a suitor by the fairytale invocation of 'once upon a time' (259). Wegg's character discourse exploits the 'sincerity' capital of poetry as a false signifier of friendship. Fiction is shown to be further corrupted in its use as ideological myth. Pupils attending ragged schools are taught the hegemonic tale of moral and material progress in the 'Adventures of Little Margery' and 'Thomas Twopence', whilst cultural mediocrity is glorified in the arts as regulated by Podsnap (214, 128).

However, the most corrupting dislocation of discourse from things as they are is represented in the text as the appropriation of the language of imaginative aspiration into the inflated artificiality of oratorical profession. If Alford was correct in diagnosing a nation whose speech had become bombastic and high-flown as not far from rapid decline, then society, as represented in the character discourse of *Our Mutual Friend*, must be in a state of almost terminal degeneration. The speech images constructed from character discourses of all sections of society reproduce the clichéd ideals of their class. On all sides, the high-flown rhetoric of hypocrisy is shown to construct a 'filmy surface' over corrupt practice, mercenary self-seeking, and predatory intent. The hollow professions of timeless friendships and intimate confidences in society compete for self-righteous honour against Riderhood's pious incantation that he gets his living by the sweat of his brow: a formula to transform the worst of treachery into proletarian virtue. Meanwhile Wegg's character discourse indulges a riot of cliché to construct a sense of high moral outrage against Boffin 'that minion of fortune and worm of the hour' (306). Mr Boffin, himself, is represented as saying, 'You have my word; and how you can have that, without my honour too, I don't know' (577), but the assertion only serves to underline the general dislocation of the two.

The effect of all the falsifying rhetorical forms imaged in character discourse is to separate words from intent, signifiers from signifieds, so that characters are depicted in a state of constant chronic suspicion as to meaning. Social language, as represented in *Our Mutual Friend*, has degenerated into a competitive power game in which high ideals and moral sentiment are the circulating currency of cynical self-interest. 'Trust' is a gambit of business bluff, 'fellow-feeling' a stratagem of politics, and 'friendship' a move in the stakes of ambition or spite. Given this corruption of the language of mutuality into a dangerous game of hostility, it is not surprising that the one speech act the text represents persistently as a genuine fusion of form and intent is that of casting people off. Old Harmon's will cuts off his family without a penny, Gaffer disowns his son, Abbey Potterson enacts the social ostracization of Gaffer and Riderhood from the Fellowship, and Charley disowns Lizzie and then Headstone. When Lizzie is represented as begging him to 'unsay those words', he reaffirms their inseparability from his intent: 'I'll not unsay them. I'll say them again . . . I have done with you. For ever, I have done with you!' (403).

The degenerative state of public discourse represented in *Our Mutual Friend* is an index of moral and cultural decline. Instead of forming the currency of communication, words enact the isolation of a competitive individualism. Within such an atomistic culture mutual friends do not exist.[9] Yet, within the textual representation of dislocated social discourse an intermittent impulse of desire for transformation is articulated. Matching the recurrence of 'as if' formulations in narrative discourse, the word 'fancy' is repeated within character discourse like a persistent return of what is repressed or denied. The word is associated most frequently with Mrs Boffin and Lizzie Hexam, but it figures even in the discourse of such cynical characters as Wrayburn and Fledgeby (236, 427). Most usually, it is involved in the articulation of an impulse of communality. Mrs Boffin 'takes a fancy' to secure the future of some orphan as a memorial of John Harmon; Lizzie Hexam's friendship with Jenny Wren is described by Charley as 'a ridiculous fancy of giving herself up to another' (100, 392). The ideological 'solution' constructed by the plot as a means of meeting this desire and of reversing cultural decline is the regenerating marriage between classes represented in the union of Lizzie Hexam and Eugene Wrayburn. It suggests the kind of revitalization of culture envisaged by Max Muller when the higher classes are forced to mix again with the lower so that the 'undercurrent' of vulgar dialects rises up 'like the waters in spring'. Sadly, although Lizzie's origin is among 'the accumulated scum' of the poorest waterside district (21), her speech image in the text is closer to Muller's 'crystal surface' of cultivated language than the recreative vigour of dialect. Her fanciful visions in the fire raise no imaginative spark in the language on the page.

It is the character discourse of Wrayburn which is proffered as the site of oppositional hegemonic values to those of the greed, self-interest, and duplicity imaged in the social discourse. Indeed, Wrayburn has been 'called' for a biblical seven years, only needing to discover 'something really worth being energetic about' (20). Wrayburn's discourse is far from representing a vulgar dialect, yet analysis of its qualities reveals promising similarities to the speech of Sam Weller. Wrayburn's character discourse articulates a persistent parodic cynicism as to the discourse of others, functioning throughout the text as an oppositional language image to the hypocritical bombast of prevailing social discourse. Moreover, the ironic protestation against the 'tyrannical humbug of your friend the bee' contains an alienated perspective rejecting the hegemonic glorification of industriousness and material accumulation (94). Like Sam Weller, Wrayburn is represented as far too quick-witted to allow himself to be interpellated into the meaning system of others. Charley Hexam is forced to address himself to Mortimer Lightwood, so totally does Wrayburn refuse to recognize his discourse. Yet, unlike the

Podsnappian speech image, Wrayburn's discourse constructs no egoistic individualistic view of himself as Absolute Subject, aimed at imposing upon others an inhibiting sense of lack. Wrayburn's discourse openly recognizes a decentred self, identity an unfathomable riddle: 'I mean so much that I – that I don't mean' (283). This lack of any stable or coherent meaning to 'I' puts the self in process, enabling a continuous, contingent invention of identity as performance.

However, it is at this point that doubt arises. Wrayburn's performances of self, as represented in the text, share nothing of the inclusive, celebratory nature of the performances of the street characters depicted in the earlier fiction. Wrayburn's theatricality exhibits no impulse to irradiate any spectators in a communal sense of comedy and glamour. On the contrary, it is characterized by a streak of sadistic disdain, materialized, most unpleasantly, in the class-based elaboration of a hunting discourse which finds enjoyment in structuring Headstone as prey. A similar tendency is evident in the inventiveness of naming. Sam Weller's use of nicknames is represented as deflating pomposity; in Wrayburn's discourse the appellations 'Mr Aaron', 'Mr Dolls', and 'Schoolmaster' have become sneeringly demeaning. The fanciful side of Wrayburn's character discourse – the references to riddles and fairytales – stays at the level of whimsy, unconnected to any real side of things as they are. Unlike Sam's tales, which mock the causal plot of moral progress with incongruity and superfluity, or Sairey's celebratory saga of the Harris family, Wrayburn's playfulness constructs no transforming comic vision of alternative values.

In the end, all the strengths of Wrayburn's discourse are negative. Even the friendship with Mortimer Lightwood, undoubtedly part of the oppositional image Wrayburn is intended to represent, is articulated more fully in Mortimer's discourse. Its effect is weakened, too, by a strain of adolescent hero-worship, suggestive of the ideology of the public school culture in which it has its origins. Indeed, despite its alienation from the hegemonic culture of Podsnap, the speech image constructed by Wrayburn's character discourse remains trapped in upper class origins, and thus is denied a material base from which to construct an alternative point of view. At its worst, this gives rise to a dehumanizing discourse which demeans women as 'dolls' and men as 'schoolmasters', and even at its baptized and regenerated best can materialize no transforming fictions of mutuality and gregariousness.

The position of Headstone as failed suitor in the plot positions him also as failed possibility within the ideological solution it constructs. In this, the text would seem more reactionary than those voices within dominant discourse which began to recognize positive qualities inhering in working-class culture. However, there is more to the representation of Bradley Headstone in the text than this. The characterization of Headstone presents, at its most intense, that desire for social transformation, shown to be engendered by poverty. Furthermore, the text hints at the potential within those of working-class origin, like Bradley Headstone, for offering new vitality to a declining culture: 'Yet there was enough of what was animal, and of what was fiery (though smouldering), still visible in him, to suggest that if young Bradley Headstone, when a pauper lad, had chanced to be told off for sea, he would not have been the last man in a ship's crew' (218). However, Headstone's desire for a life beyond the enclosing poverty of waterside streets seeks escape, not at sea, but through the education provided for poor boys in the national schools. The text of *Great Expectations* offers a previsionary exploration of the containment of social discontent in the dreams of consumer plenitude. In *Our Mutual Friend*, the story of the Boffins, as part of the 'solution' offered, recognizes this function of consumerism, but without the critical focus of *Great Expectations*.[10] In *Our Mutual Friend* it is the mediation of desire into educational aspiration which is brought under scrutiny. Again this is previsionary. The education reforms begun in the early 1860s, leading to improved standards in public schools and to compulsory primary education for the working class in 1872, reflected a shift of attitude among the well-to-do. Increasingly, as religion lost its influence, education was turned to as the main means of sustaining the existing social order, becoming the most effective of all ideological apparatuses. The character discourses of Wrayburn and Headstone in the text provide speech images of the two education systems: the one inculcating a disdainful superiority, the other an inarticulate self-doubt. These two voices were to continue unchanged through into this present century.

Towards the end of the novel, Headstone is represented as saying: 'I am a man who has lived a retired life. I have no resources beyond myself. I have absolutely no friends' (799). The speech image constructed by his discourse conveys this impoverished perspective. Wrayburn designates Headstone's speech 'a catechizing infection' and the text provides an image of this approved regimented discourse performed by rote in the national schools. Miss Peacher uses the question and answer routine to seal off in its closed form any dangerous reality beyond established fact (220–1). No 'as if' formulations are allowed into this discourse to open out a space for the inventiveness of desire. Bradley Headstone is the last representation in Dickens's completed fiction of a boy reared in the city streets, and what a painful sense of diminishment there is in this characterization when it is compared to that of Sam Weller. Headstone's rejection of shameful origins is represented as a loss also of the class vitality they produce. Absent from his discourse are the street wit, the spontaneous theatricality, and the conviviality of the earlier street characters. Headstone's cumbrous 'educated' language falls easily into the traps set by the aggressive word games of Wrayburn and Riderhood. His discourse is bereft of the comic and fanciful inventiveness by means of which Wrayburn is able to create an imaginative spaciousness in the midst of Lizzie Hexam's straitened life. Neither is it shown to have the capacity to articulate a language of desire. Sexual love is expressed without joy, wholly as a threat to social identity. Frequently his discourse confesses bitterly to its own impotence and lack: 'Whatever I say to you seems, even in my ears, below what I want to say, and different from what I want to say' (395). Rote education has dislocated Headstone's words from his own passion and desire.

What is most noticeably lost, also, is any capacity for playful self-invention. Desire for transformation of a pauper identity has been mediated wholly into the ego-ideal of respectability. His discourse elaborates no image of self beyond the closure of this rigid social model. His 'decent' clothes and his subdued habit signify equally with his guarded speech a total conformity to the social ideal. Even the need to present himself in persuasive terms to Lizzie Hexam falls back upon reiteration of professional competence and status: 'If you saw me at my work, able to do it well and respected in it, you might even come to take a sort of pride in me' (397). The proliferation of modifiers, 'If', 'might', 'even', 'sort', denies even the meagre confidence of this impoverished assertion of self. It represents a conception of identity reduced to the fixed term 'schoolmaster', with the possibility of playful elaboration 'subdued to the performance of his routine of educational tricks' (546). Bradley Headstone is a representation of the totally taught and regimented self.

His character discourse returns obsessively to the hegemonic lesson of moral progress expounded assiduously in schools for the working class. Self-discipline and repression earn the right to respectable status, 'the right to be considered a better man ... with better reasons for being proud' (293). However, the compulsive repetition of this claim is a register of insecurity. Status based upon denial of origins is inevitably an implicit confession of lack. In the indolent class gaze of Wrayburn, with 'its cold disdain of him as a creature of no worth', the sense of distance from the desired self is mirrored back (288). The more the assured image is confronted, the more intensely the unsure, taught self is registered as bereft of social esteem, and as cheated and deluded by the hegemonic myth. All interpellations of margin to centre, subject to Absolute Subject contain this socially dangerous potential for alienation. Desire for identification with an Absolute Ego-Ideal inevitable involves a simultaneous registering of self as lacking; this can effect a slippage of desire into a libidinous impulse to violate and destroy the image which was first sought. Headstone's murderous attempt to smash the image which mirrors his lack thus represents a simultaneous act of self-destruction, and wiping his name from the school blackboard fittingly acknowledges the erasure of his taught and only identity. The passion of anger in Headstone is represented as wholly negative, constructing no alternative perspective, and the despairing return to origins in the slime and mud of the riverbed is devoid of regenerative impulse. The complex psychological characterization of Headstone thus represents a dialogic challenge to those ideas of 'civilized' evolution current in dominant discourse. The struggling aspiring energies of the working class in the poorest waterside districts are presented in the text as a potential source of regenerative vigour to national culture, rather than as the feared source of degeneration. However, the education provided for the poor is not shown, in *Our Mutual Friend*, as a bulwark against descent into 'savagery'. On the contrary, savagery is presented as the underside of 'civilized' evolution – the effect of the repressions it exerts.

Jenny Wren's visionary promise 'Come up and be dead' chimes dialogically against Headstone's insisted 'Come down' (282, 802). This is not the only oppositional interaction of their discourses. Jenny Wren's speech image is characterized by an alert readiness to anger. Unlike that of Headstone, her anger is presented as a strategy of survival in a tough predatory world in which 'they don't care for you, those fellows, if you're not hard upon 'em', and where mutual friendship more usually masks hostile intent. As such, her sharpness of speech, like that of Sairey Gamp, articulates a positive assertion of self-worth; that she is the 'person of the house' and not to be deceived or set at naught. This is in total contrast to Headstone's destructive rage, depicted as the effect of self-negation and loss. Her anger is represented as a regenerating response to the material conditions of a childhood, 'chilled, anxious, ragged, beaten, . . . [and] in pain' – as if 'the sharpness of the manner seemed unavoidable' (239). This origin of anger in hardship and oppression spreads outward from self-assertion to an indignant fellow-feeling for others experiencing privation or injustice. In the text, it is only Jenny Wren's discourse of friendship which fuses profession with an aggressive intent to act on behalf of those, like Lizzie and Riah, for whom she is concerned. The positive strength of her anger is presented as stemming from its roots in the material conditions of poverty; the negativity of Headstone's in the loss of self-esteem through rejection of those regenerative origins.

Jenny Wren's discourse also images the sharp wisdom of street culture. The 'tricks and manners' of 'all those fellows', including those of Wrayburn who is able to play such games upon Headstone's dullness, are always counterpointed and mocked in her speech. In any language game, as in the encounter with Fledgeby, she is depicted as always several moves ahead. Her parody of submissive response. 'Can't undertake to say, sir', checkmates Fledgeby's questioning at every turn, whilst she shrewdly interrogates his language for the intent it unwittingly reveals (716). Her discourse is characterized also by a 'catechizing' habit, a parody of the schoolteacher routine, but unlike Miss Peacher's evasive formulations, Jenny Wren's sharp little questions always move towards an ironic probing of intent underlying surface profession, as in the representation of her quizzing Headstone on his 'disinterested' motives in coming to see Lizzie (342). In its multiple resourcefulness, its hard-bitten cynicism as to intentions behind rhetoric, and its positive impulse of anger – all qualities originating in a material class point of view – the speech image constructed by Jenny Wren's character discourse achieves a more powerful and convincing counterforce than that of Wrayburn's to the social chorus of bombast and deceit.

As this suggests, it is the 'vulgar' discourse of Jenny Wren's speech image which is the locus of a positive, non-hegemonic, perspective based upon material cultural practice and which engages in a sustained dialogic critique of the imaginary solutions offered by the plot structure. Along with sharpness, Jenny Wren's character discourse articulates a pervasive impulse for inventive transformation. Her language constantly inscribes what is ordinary, shabby or even pathetic with a playful glamour. Thus her crutch becomes a 'carriage', Riah a 'fairy godmother', and scrambling amidst the traffic of the street for a glimpse of fashionable ladies is named 'trying on'. This is an imaginative remaking of necessity, not the escape from it represented in the consumer stylishness of the Boffin/Bella mansion. Moreover, unlike Wrayburn's naming and whimsy, Jenny Wren's transformative discourse is always inclusive, inviting others into the playful arena of the imagination. The most sustained act of naming is self-naming. As 'Jenny Wren' her 'character' discourse remakes and performs self with a creative energy which holds defiantly at bay any perception of a piteous actuality. In this performance of self even 'queer legs' and 'bad back' are brought into the control of the speaking subject's own ironic self-representation, and thus withheld from the mockery or pity of the discourse of others. The 'person of the house' so interpellates herself that she can never be constructed (taught) by anyone as a doll in a doll's house. However, despite this fictionalization of self, her discourse, like Sairey Gamp's, is marked by an insistent return to the material necessity of working for a living. 'You may take it for granted' she is represented as telling Fledgeby, 'that it's always worth my while to make money' (717).

The same binding connection between imaginative transformation and 'things as they are' structures the fiction of her drunken father as bad child. In this, the text constructs a shaming contrast between the greedy appetite of the wealthy for sensational stories of human distress as source of frivolous entertainment, and the desperate inventive strategies of the poor for securing a perception of affection and self-respect in the face of degenerative degradation. Jenny Wren's discourse of scolding and threat constructs a fable of youthful misbehaviour enacted against the persistent presence of an angry but anxious and caring parent; a transformation of sordid actuality into its reverse. However, this does not involve evasion of reality; indeed her words generalize the dangers and pain inherent in the working-class culture of the streets, now as then: 'You see it is so hard to bring up a child well, when you work, work, work, all day. When he was out of employment, I couldn't always keep him near me. He got fractious and nervous, and I was obliged to let him go into the streets. And he never did well in the streets, he never did well out of sight' (732). This insisted reality inscribed in Jenny Wren's character discourse undermines those consoling gestures of the ideological plot – the patronage of Betty Higden and Sloppy. In the words of *The Times*, these latter are shown to partake of 'the charity of the guinea list' rather than growing out of the actualities 'of dear life itself'.

Furthermore, the play upon the word 'doll' in association with the characterization of Jenny Wren produces an effect of condensation upon that image which points to hidden ideological ambiguities linking together the Lizzie/Wrayburn and the Bella/Harmon plot 'solutions'. Jenny Wren's work in the streets is part of the impulse for playful transformation. In opposition to the 'national dread of colour' (393) under the moral regime of Podsnappian conformity, Jenny's dolls present a 'dazzling semi-circle . . . in all the colours of the rainbow', that symbol of a promised renewal reconnecting earth to heaven (435). However, the worker, the producer of the dolls, which are dressed up 'for all the gay events of life' (435), has never played and her body is deformed as a degenerating effect of poverty. From this ironic perspective the dolls must be recognized as parodies not only of Lady Tippens (made and unmade night and morning), but also of Bella's love of dressing up and of Mrs Boffin's consumer dream of being 'a highflyer at Fashion' (55). It was notorious that the ostentatious display of fashionable dresses at 'gay events', like those catalogued and priced by Lady Tippens at the Lammles' wedding, were produced by dressmakers whose health was crippled by their conditions of work and by the privations imposed by starvation wages. These wages made dressmakers and seamstresses, like Lizzie Hexam, a well-known source of purchasable sex for cynical men about town.[11] During the 1860s, the controversy over the Contagious Diseases Act, which instituted compulsory medical examination of prostitutes, constructed another strand to that public discourse upon national decline and corruption. In this context, 'setting up a doll' has only one meaning; prostitutes dressed in the trashy finery of cheap consumer taste, like one of Jenny Wren's 'flaunting dolls' (731), offered an easily purchased escape from the hypocritical social regimen of the Podsnappian 'young person'. The showy surface of conspicuous consumer display was linked to its undercurrent of defilement by harsh bonds of economic necessity. In this way, the ambiguous image of Jenny's dolls contains the promise of a visionary transforming energy of productivity and playfulness, which is, at the same time, represented as abused and defiled by the class which exploits and breaks it.

This radical hidden class-consciousness is recontained by the absorption of Jenny Wren into the elect circle of wealthy patronage: those who 'have great power of doing good to others' (680). The plot attempts to cage Jenny Wren like one of the 'cultivated' birds in the expensive aviary in the Boffin mansion, the description of which reads like an inventory of luxurious consumer display (767). Throughout the text of *Our Mutual Friend*, discontent (even hatred) with things as they are is registered in a desire for transformation, split between imaginative remaking and a tired escape from the need to struggle. This latter retreat from reality is materialized in the ascent to privileged consumer contentment away from all 'girding' voices at the novel's conclusion. The split is reproduced also in the characterization of Jenny Wren: in the falsifying sentimentality of her religious rhapsodies and her siren song 'Come up and be dead'. Although from the dislocating perspective of the rooftops, Jenny only pities the 'people who are alive, crying and working and calling to one another down in the close dark streets' (281), the language of that statement undercuts its apparent assertion of disconnection from that world. As always, her character discourse testifies to the vitality and mutuality of working-class origins. Only the culture of 'common' streets and work creates that transforming vision of new life which yet retains living contact with material reality – the interconnection of 'as' with 'if'.

Early in the novel, Silas Wegg, setting out to exploit language, imaginative aspiration, friendship, and gregariousness for fraudulent gain, encounters 'Eddard' the donkey and his owner, the hoarse gentleman. By them he is engaged as participant in a spontaneous performance of comic and radiant superfluity. ' "Keep yer hi on his ears," says the hoarse gentleman, and he, the hind hoofs, the truck, and Edward, all seemed to fly into the air together, in a kind of apotheosis' (55). This snatch of 'vulgar dialect' offers a theatrical image of transformation and communality, which, despite decades of inculcation of individualistic competitiveness and educational conformism, has its origins in a resilient oppositional working-class point of view. It is a voice possibly speaking still and laughing in our common streets, and offering the option of a radically regenerating mutuality.

Notes

1. This led to the Revised Code of Education which came into operation in June 1863, establishing the principle of 'payment by results' for teachers and thus increasing the pressure on them to teach by rote. Philip Collins in *Dickens and Education* (1963), although rather unsympathetic to the presentation of Headstone, gives helpful information on the social status of national school teachers, pp. 159–71.

2. The *Christian Observer* expressed this unease in the prevailing discourse of evolution: 'A people bent on amusement is either emerging from a savage, or declining into an exhausted state ... when the populace demanded nothing but feasts and spectacles, Rome was hastening to decay ... we see many painful symptoms of this degeneracy in the present state of England' (1864, p. 408).

3. In an account of the prevalence of fraud, *The Times* (25 April 1863) referred to the representation of commercial dishonesty in Dickens's

early fiction. In fact, the confidence trickster described in the *Times* article as imposing on friends by telling them that his house in Belgrave Square was in the hands of upholsterers and that 'there was no telling when those decorators would have done with so magnificent a mansion' seems very close indeed to the depiction of Alfred Lammle in *Our Mutual Friend*.

4. It is impossible here to give an accurate impression of the dispersed and varied nature of this turning towards forms of mutuality within dominant discourse; it ranges from widespread praise for the mutual help among the Lancashire cotton workers during the disastrous effects on the industry of the American Civil War, to a letter in the *Spectator* asserting the higher obligation of social principle after fifty years experience of self-interest (17 August 1861), to a speaker at the Social Science Congress of 1863 advocating more amusement for the working class, since 'laughter is essentially a social, a sympathetic, and a contagious power' (*The Times*, 14 October 1863).

5. Reading the many reviews of the continuous stream of archeological and geological books being published in the 1860s helps to make this parodic intent more obvious. For example, a typical review in the *Westminster Review* described a geological finding thus: 'Among these cinders . . . [and] among the ashes . . . were a great variety of bones and implements' (79 (1863), p. 543). Contemptuous references to 'raking in the dust' were commonplace at the time among those who opposed evolutionary theories. In the contentious atmosphere aroused by Darwin's claims, his 'scientific' supporters were vociferous in depicting themselves as proponents of 'progress' and 'reason' — active in forwarding national evolution onto an even higher scale, as opposed to the entrenched 'superstition' of religious conservatism. Undoubtedly, Veneering's gloomy analytical chemist would place himself among the adherents of 'progress'.

6. In fact, *The Times* was more eloquent and less sentimental than Dickens in depicting the plight of the poor. For example, in its number for 14 November 1863, it printed a long editorial describing a pitiful scene outside the workhouse of St Martin's-in-the-Fields, where about forty people 'huddled together for mutual warmth and the consoling touch of fellow-suffering'. Most were turned away into a bitter night, submitting to their fate 'in passive despair'. *The Times* concluded 'such a scene as we have just described ought to be impossible in this rich and luxurious city . . . it is plain inhumanity to let a human creature starve with cold and hunger'.

7. See, for example, pp. 29–30, 41, 53, 99–100, 406.

8. Of course, I am not suggesting that Dickens does not use such formulations (which include a repeated use of the verb 'to seem' as well as 'as if' and 'as though') in other texts, simply that in *Our Mutual Friend*

these usages are foregrounded by their frequency.

9. Perhaps Dickens knew that Henry Alford had declared that grammatically there was no such person as 'a mutual friend'! (*Christian Observer*, 1864, p. 620).

10. In fact, Mr and Mrs Boffin's consumer delight (pp. 100, 466) shown as an imaginative expansive reaction to their earlier life of unremitting drudgery, is part of the text's positive underwriting of desire for transformation in the poor. Only as the novel progresses does escape into consumer luxury become a substitute for genuine transformative energy.

11. One of the most remarkable examples of the changed attitude to mutuality, referred to earlier in the chapter, was an article in *The Times* supporting an attempt to unionize dressmakers and milliners, so that 'the workwomen can combine to demand what is right for themselves'. Only by thus improving their conditions, it was argued, would they be protected 'against temptations of a certain kind' (3 September 1863).

Afterword

Although Dickens's novels are discussed in chronological order, I began and continued my readings with the conscious intention of constructing no master narrative of Dickens's development, either in terms of theme or artistic practice. What I wanted to focus upon and to document was the synchronic relation of individual texts with their particular moment of history, their absolutely up-to-the-minute involvement with the ongoing discourse of class, rather than any internal continuities from one to another. Having this aim in mind, I tried to approach all the texts – Dickens's and the various journals – as nearly as possible without preconceptions; to let coincidences of their imagery, language choices and issues alert me to the common ideological struggles and debate sited in them all as a response to material events in the world. Only when I was writing the penultimate chapter did I begin to realize that I was, after all, telling a story. However, this narrative is not intrinsic to Dickens's fiction; it is simply the narrative of social change inscribed, inevitably, in the discourses of the time. What is traced is the elaboration of increasingly sophisticated mechanisms of interpellative control, in response to the changing needs of capitalist organization. During the period of wrenching social change which inaugurated the competitive capitalism of the early nineteenth century, the crisis of resulting unrest was met by systematic interpellation of all potential discontents – the have-nots – as guilty, inadequate subjects. This repressive mechanism was not abandoned with increased prosperity after 1850 (although the apparatus shifted from religion to education), but the need to stimulate economic demand favoured an emphasis on interpellation as consumer promise. While it would be difficult to tell this story from Dickens's texts alone, they are an essential means of telling it most fully. Only there can we hear now those silenced oppositional voices of the marginalized who did not submit to this process without articulating its pain and their anger. However, literature does not only construct speech images of those social voices speaking in its era; more than any other form of discourse, it takes the imprint of desire. By its nature, desire – utopianism – is unrealistic; it always risks an escapist turning-away from present difficulty and lack, but without it we deny ourselves the energy and imagination we need to be the makers of our own future narrative.

Bibliography

This is not an attempt at a comprehensive or exhaustive list of references to the subject of this book; it is simply a compilation of works consulted and/or referred to in this text. For convenience I have divided it into two sections: one for studies of Dickens and the other general. The place of publication is London unless stated otherwise.

1. Dickens

Auden, W. H., 'Dingley Dell & The Fleet', in *The Dyer's Hand and Other Essays* (Faber, 1963), pp. 407–28.

Blount, Trevor, 'Dickens's Slum Satire in *Bleak House*', *Modern Language Review*, 60 (1965), pp. 340–51.

Blount, Trevor, 'Poor Jo, Education, and the Problem of Juvenile Delinquency', *Modern Philology*, 62 (1965), pp. 325–39.

Blount, Trevor, 'The Chadbands and Dickens' View of Dissenters', *Modern Language Quarterly*, 25 (1964), pp. 295–307.

Brook, G. L., *The Language of Dickens* (André Deutsch, 1970).

Butt, John and Tillotson, Kathleen, *Dickens at Work* (Methuen, 1957).

Carey, John, *The Violent Effigy* (Faber, 1973).

Chase, Karen, *The Representation of Personality in Charlotte Bronte, Charles Dickens and George Eliot* (Methuen, 1984).

Chesterton, G. K., *Charles Dickens* (Methuen, 1906).

Clark, Cumberland, *Dickens and Democracy and other studies* (Cecil Palmer, 1930).

Collins, Philip, *Dickens and Crime* (Macmillan, 1962).

Collins, Philip, *Dickens and Education* (Macmillan, 1963).

Collins, Philip, 'Dickens and Industrialism', *Studies in English Literature*, 20 (1980), pp. 653–73.

Eigner, Edwin M., 'Death and the Gentleman: *David Copperfield* as Elegiac Romance', *Dickens Studies Annual*, 16 (1987), pp. 39–59.

Fielding, K. J., *Charles Dickens: A Critical Introduction* (Longmans, 1965).

Ford, G. H., *Dickens and his Readers* (Princeton, New Jersey: Princeton University Press, 1955).

Forster, John, *Life of Charles Dickens*, ed. A. J. Hoppe, 2 vols (Dent, 1966).

Frank, Lawrence, *Charles Dickens and the Romantic Self* (Lincoln: University of Nebraska Press, 1984).

Garis, Robert, *The Dickens Theatre: A Reassessment of the Novels* (Oxford: Clarendon Press, 1965).

Gissing, George, *Charles Dickens: A Critical Study* (Blackie, 1898).

Hardy, Barbara, *The Moral Art of Dickens* (Athlone Press, 1970).

Hardy, Barbara, *Dickens: The Later Novels* (Longman, 1977).

Hollington, Michael, *Dickens and the Grotesque* (Croom Helm, 1984).

House, Humphrey, *The Dickens World*, 2nd edn (Oxford University Press, 1942).

Humphreys, Ann, 'Dickens and Mayhew on the London Poor', *Dickens Studies Annual*, 4 (1975), pp. 78–90.

Jackson, T. A., *Dickens: Progress of a Radical* (Lawrence & Wishart, 1937).

Johnson, Edgar, *Charles Dickens: His Tragedy and Triumph*, 2 vols (New York, Simon & Schuster, 1952).

Kettle, Arnold, 'Charles Dickens: The Novelist and the People', *Marxism Today*, February, 1963, pp. 48–54.

Kincaid, J. R., *Dickens and the Rhetoric of Laughter* (Oxford University Press, 1971).

Kincaid, J. R., 'Viewing and Blurring in Dickens: The Misrepresentation of Representation', *Dickens Studies Annual*, 16 (1987), pp. 94–111.

Kucich, John, 'Repression and Representation: Dickens's General Economy', *Nineteenth-Century Fiction*, 38 (1983), pp. 62–77.

Leavis, F. R., and Q. D., *Dickens the Novelist* (Chatto & Windus, 1970).

Lindsay, Jack, *Charles Dickens: A Biographical and Critical Study* (Dakers, 1950).

Lucas, John, *The Melancholy Man: A Study of Dickens's Novels* (Methuen, 1970).

Magnet, Myron, *Dickens and Social Order* (Philadelphia: University of Pennsylvania Press, 1985).

Marcus, Stephen, *Dickens: From Pickwick to Dombey* (Chatto & Windus, 1965).

Miller, J. Hillis, *Charles Dickens: The World of His Novels* (Cambridge, Mass.: Harvard University Press, 1968).

Nelson, Harland, S., 'Dickens's *Our Mutual Friend* and Mayhew's *London Labour and London Poor*', *Nineteenth-Century Fiction*, 20 (1965), pp. 207–22.

Newman, S. J., *Dickens at Play* (Macmillan, 1981).

Orwell, George, 'Charles Dickens' in *Inside the Whale* (Gollancz, 1940).

Pakenham, Pansy, 'Dickens and the Class Question', *Victorian Newsletter*, 16 (1959), p. 30.

Pugh, Edwin, *The Dickens Originals*, (T. N. Foulis, 1913).

Schlicke, Paul, *Dickens and Popular Entertainment* (Allen & Unwin, 1985).

Smith, Sheila, 'John Overs to Charles Dickens: A Working Man's Letter and its implications', *Victorian Studies*, 18 (1974), pp. 195–217.

Spector, Stephen J., 'Monsters of Metonymy: *Hard Times* and Knowing the Working Class', *ELH*, 51 (1984), pp. 365–84.

Stewart, Garrett, *Dickens and the Trials of Imagination* (Cambridge, Mass.: Harvard University Press, 1974).

Sucksmith, H. P., 'Sir Leicester Dedlock, Wat Tyler and the Chartists: The

Role of the Ironmaster in *Bleak House*', *Dickens Studies Annual*, 4 (1975), pp. 113–31.

Tambling, Jeremy, 'Prison-bound: Dickens and Foucault', *Essays in Criticism*, 36 (1986), pp. 11–31.

Walder, Dennis, *Dickens and Religion* (Allen & Unwin, 1981).

Welsh, Alexander, *The City of Dickens* (Oxford: Clarendon Press, 1971).

Welsh, Alexander, *From Copyright to Copperfield: The Identity of Dickens* (Cambridge, Mass.: Harvard University Press, 1987).

Wilson, Angus, *The World of Charles Dickens* (Harmondsworth, Middlesex: Penguin, 1972).

Wilson, Edmund, 'Dickens: The Two Scrooges', in *The Wound and the Bow* (Methuen, 1961).

2. General

Althusser, Louis, *Essays on Ideology* (Verso, 1984).

Arnold, Matthew, *Culture and Anarchy* [1869] (Cambridge University Press, 1932).

Bakhtin, Mikhail, *Rabelais and His World*, trans. Helene Iswolsky (Cambridge, Mass.: MIT Press, 1968).

Bakhtin, Mikhail, *The Dialogic Imagination: Four Essays* ed. Michael Holquist, trans. C. Emerson & M. Holquist (Austin: University of Texas Press, 1981).

Balibar, Etienne, and Macherey, Pierre, 'On Literature as an Ideological Form' in *Untying the Text*, ed. Robert Young (Routledge & Kegan Paul, 1981).

Bamford, Samuel, *Autobiography of Samuel Bamford* [1839–41, 1848–9] ed. W. H. Chaloner, 2 vols (Frank Cass, 1967).

Best, Geoffrey, *Mid-Victorian Britain 1851–70* (Fontana, 1979).

Bottomore, T. B., *Classes in Modern Society*, (Allen & Unwin, 1965).

Bradley, Ian, *The Call to Seriousness: The Evangelical Impact on the Victorians* (Jonathan Cape, 1976).

Briggs, Asa, *Victorian Cities* (Harmondsworth, Middlesex: Penguin, 1968).

Briggs, Asa, and Saville, John, ed. *Essays in Labour History* (Macmillan, 1960).

Burnett, John, ed., *Useful Toil: Autobiographies of Working People from the 1820s to the 1920s* (Harmondsworth, Middlesex: Penguin, 1977).

Carlyle, Thomas, 'Chartism' [1839] in *Selected Essays* (Dent, 1972).

Cazamian, Louis, *The Social Novel in England 1830–1850*, trans. Martin Fido (Routledge & Kegan Paul, 1973).

Cole, G. D. H., *Studies in Class Structure* (Routledge & Kegan Paul, 1955).

Cunningham, Valentine, *Everywhere Spoken Against: Dissent in the Victorian Novel* (Oxford: Clarendon Press, 1975).

Deleuze, Gilles, and Guattari, Felix, *Anti-Oedipus: Capitalism and Schizophrenia*, trans. R. Hurley, M. Seem and H. R. Lane (Athlone Press, 1984).

Eagleton, Mary, and Pierce, David, *Attitudes to Class in the English Novel: From Walter Scott to David Storey* (Thames & Hudson, 1979).

Engels, Frederick, *The Condition of the Working Class in England* [1845] (Frogmore, St Albans, Herts.: Panther, 1969).

Faber, Richard, *Proper Stations; Class in Victorian Fiction* (Faber, 1971).

Foucault, Michel, *Discipline and Punish: The Birth of the Prison*, trans. Alan Sheridan (Allen Lane, 1977).

Foucault, Michel, *The History of Sexuality: An Introduction*, vol 1, trans. Robert Hurley (Allen Lane, 1979).

Foucault, Michel, 'The Order of Discourse' in *Untying the Text*, ed. Robert Young (Routledge & Kegan Paul, 1981).

Freud, Sigmund, *Beyond the Pleasure Principle*, Pelican Freud Library, vol 11 (Harmondsworth, Middlesex: Penguin, 1984).

Freud, Sigmund, *Civilization and Its Discontents*, Pelican Freud Library, vol 12 (Harmondsworth, Middlesex: Penguin, 1985).

Gilbert, Alan D., *Religion and Society in Industrial England* (Longman, 1976).

Gilmore, Robin, *The Idea of the Gentleman in the Victorian Novel* (Allen & Unwin, 1981).

Hammond, J. L., and Barbara, *The Town Labourer* [1917], ed. John Lovell (Longman, 1978).

Harrison, Fraser, *The Dark Angel: Aspects of Victorian Sexuality* (Sheldon Press, 1977).

Harrison, J. F. C., *Early Victorian Britain* (Fontana, 1979).

Hoggart, Richard, *The Uses of Literacy* (Harmondsworth, Middlesex: Penguin, 1958).

Hollis, Patricia, ed., *Class and Conflict in Nineteenth-Century England 1815–1850* (Routledge & Kegan Paul, 1973).

Hopkinson, James, *Victorian Cabinet Maker: The Memoirs of James Hopkinson 1819–1894*, ed. Jocelyn Baty Goodman (Routledge & Kegan Paul, 1968).

Jackson, Brian, and Marsden, Dennis, *Education and the Working Class* (Harmondsworth, Middlesex: Penguin, 1966).

James, Louis, *Fiction for the Working Man* (Oxford University Press, 1963).

James, Louis, *Print and the People* (Oxford University Press, 1963).

James, Louis, 'The View from Brick Lane: Contrasting Perspectives in Working-Class and Middle-Class Fiction of the Early Victorian Period', *The Year Book of English Studies*, 2 (1981), pp. 87–101.

Jameson, Fredric, *The Political Unconscious: Narrative as a Socially Symbolic Act* (Methuen, 1981).

Jay, Elizabeth, *The Religion of the Heart: Anglican Evangelicalism in the Nineteenth-Century Novel* (Oxford: Clarendon Press, 1979).

Keating, Peter, *The Working Class in Victorian Fiction* (Routledge & Kegan Paul, 1971).

Kristeva, Julia, *Desire in Language: A Semiotic Approach to Literature and Art*, ed. Leon S. Roudiez, trans. T. Gora, A. Jardine and L. S. Roudiez (Blackwell,

1981).

Kristeva, Julia, *Powers of Horror*, trans. Leon S. Roudiez (New York: Columbia University Press, 1982).

Kristeva, Julia, 'A Question of Subjectivity', *Women's Review*, 12 (1986), pp. 19–21.

Lacan, Jacques, *Ecrits: A Selection*, trans. Alan Sheridan (Tavistock Publications, 1977).

Laclau, Ernesto, *Politics and Ideology in Marxist Theory* (Verso, 1979).

Leavis, Q. D., *Fiction and the Reading Public* (Chatto & Windus, 1932).

Llewellyn Davis, Margaret, ed., *Life As We Have Known It* [1931] (Virago, 1977).

Lovett, William, *Life and Struggles of William Lovett* [1876] (Garland, 1984).

Macherey, Pierre, *A Theory of Literary Production*, trans. Geoffrey Wall (Routledge & Kegan Paul, 1978). and Balibar, Etienne, 'On Literature as an Ideological Form' in *Untying the Text*, ed. Robert Young (Routledge & Kegan Paul, 1981).

Marcus, Stephen, *The Other Victorians: A Study of Sexuality and Pornography in Mid-Nineteenth-Century England* (Weidenfeld & Nicolson, 1967).

Marcus, Stephen, *Engels, Manchester and the Working Class* (Weidenfeld & Nicolson, 1974).

Marshall, J. D., *The Old Poor Law 1795–1834* (Macmillan, 1968).

Mayhew, Henry, *London Labour and London Poor*, 4 vols (New York: Dover Publications, 1968).

Meacham, Standish, *A Life Apart: The English Working Class 1890–1914* (Thames & Hudson, 1971).

Miall, E., *The British Churches in Relation to the British People* (A. Hall, Virtue, 1849).

Nesbitt, George L., *Benthamite Reviewing: The First Twelve Years of the Westminster Review* (New York: Columbia University Press, 1934).

Perkin, Harold, *The Origins of Modern English Society 1780–1880* (Routledge & Kegan Paul, 1972).

Quinlan, Maurice J., *Victorian Prelude: A History of English Manners 1700–1830* (New York: Columbia University Press, 1941).

Rose, Michael E., *The Relief of Poverty 1834–1914* (Macmillan, 1972).

Ruskin, John, *Unto This Last* [1862] (Harmondsworth, Middlesex: Penguin, 1985).

Said, Edward W., *The World, the Text, and the Critic* (Faber, 1984).

Smiles, Samuel, *Self-Help* [1859] (John Murray, 1958).

Thompson, E. P., *The Making of the English Working Class* (Harmondsworth, Middlesex: Penguin, 1968).

Thompson, E. P., 'Eighteenth-Century English Society: Class Struggle without Class?' *Social History*, 3 (1978), pp. 133–65.

Thompson, E. P., and Yeo, Eileen, ed., *The Unknown Mayhew* (Merlin Press, 1971).

Thompson, Flora, *Lark Rise to Candleford* [1939–43] (Harmondsworth, Middlesex: Penguin, 1973).

Thompson, F. M. L., *English Landed Gentry in the Nineteenth Century* (Routledge & Kegan Paul, 1963).

Thompson, F. M. L., *Rise of Respectable Society* (Fontana, 1988).

Thompson, Paul, 'Voices from Within' in *The Victorian City* ed. H. J. Dyos and Michael Wolff, 2 vols (Routledge & Kegan Paul, 1973), I, pp. 59–80.

Tillotson, Kathleen, *Novels of the Eighteen-Forties* (Oxford: Clarendon Press, 1954).

Webb, R. K., *Modern England: From the Eighteenth Century to the Present* (Allan & Unwin, 1969).

Wiener, Martin J., *English Culture and the Decline of the Industrial Spirit 1850–1980* (Cambridge University Press, 1982).

Williams, Raymond, *Culture and Society 1780–1950* (Harmondsworth, Middlesex: Penguin, 1963).

Williams, Raymond, *The English Novel from Dickens to Lawrence* (Chatto & Windus, 1970).

Williams, Raymond, *Marxism and Literature* (Oxford: Oxford University Press, 1977).

Wright, Thomas, *The Great Unwashed* (Tinsley Brothers, 1868).

Young, G. M., *Victorian England: Portrait of an Age* (Oxford University Press, 1936).

Index